Understanding Child and Family Welfare

Understanding Child and Family Welfare

Statutory Responses to Children at Risk

MARIE CONNOLLY AND KATE MORRIS

First published 2012 by
PALGRAVE MACMILLAN

Palgrave Macmillan in the UK is an imprint of Macmillan Publishers Limited,
registered in England, company number 785998, of Houndmills, Basingstoke,
Hampshire RG21 6XS.

Palgrave Macmillan in the US is a division of St Martin's Press LLC,
175 Fifth Avenue, New York, NY 10010.

Palgrave Macmillan is the global academic imprint of the above companies
and has companies and representatives throughout the world.

Palgrave® and Macmillan® are registered trademarks in the United States,
the United Kingdom, Europe and other countries.

ISBN-13: 978–0–230–25019–2

This book is printed on paper suitable for recycling and made from fully
managed and sustained forest sources. Logging, pulping and manufacturing
processes are expected to conform to the environmental regulations of the
country of origin.

A catalogue record for this book is available from the British Library.

A catalog record for this book is available from the Library of Congress.

10 9 8 7 6 5 4 3 2 1
21 20 19 18 17 16 15 14 13 12

Printed and bound in Great Britain by
CPI Antony Rowe, Chippenham and Eastbourne

Contents

List of Tables and Figures

Preface

Child protection and family support practice is constantly evolving in response to contemporary challenges and concerns. Workers in child and family welfare make some of the most difficult decisions that the state has to make, often with far-reaching consequences for children and their families. In recent decades demand for statutory child protection services in English speaking jurisdictions has continued to rise and systems have been exposed to considerable scrutiny, particularly when tragedy occurs. In response, most systems have undergone review and reform. Whilst some reform efforts have produced positive results, many well-intentioned reforms have struggled to achieve the anticipated outcomes – a conundrum that the recent Munro Review in England (2010) is seeking to understand.

In this book we look at the ways in which child welfare systems respond to the needs of children and families in this contemporary and contested environment. Whilst we look at services for children across a number of jurisdictions it is not our intention to compare one against another. Countries have their own ways of defining abuse and neglect, and they have their own unique ways of responding to family issues. Alternatively, we explore innovative frameworks, approaches and key ideas that have emerged primarily from jurisdictions that have responded to similar challenges in providing responsive services for children. To illustrate the breadth of innovative practices we have drawn examples from a number of countries that will be more or less familiar depending on where you live and work. We hope you will enjoy exploring these various international experiences and that you find the similarities and differences of equal interest and significance.

We begin the book in Chapter 1 by considering changing attitudes to children and childhood, child-rearing and parenting. We look at stressors that impact on children and their families, including poverty, parental conflict and violence, and issues of mental health, and then consider the development of professional knowledge with respect to child maltreatment. Whilst child abuse and neglect has the clear potential to impact negatively on life outcomes, we also look at what contributes to good outcomes for children. Positive parenting, a stable family life, and a supportive family and community network can become protective factors for children. The chapter explores what is understood by 'well-being', how children and families confront adversity, and how experiences can either create the context for the development of new skills and strengths, or result in ongoing trauma and pain.

Chapter 2 then considers differing philosophical orientations to child welfare: child protection and family support orientation. Each is influenced by a set of beliefs and understandings about the state/ family relationship and the needs of children and each informs regulatory frameworks that create responses to children at risk. We look at differential responses to child protection, and ways in which services have sought to provide responses based on what families actually need. Developing alternative pathways for families has been a popular service reform across international jurisdictions, and we finish the chapter by looking at the ways in which child protection services are constantly evolving within a dynamic and often politically charged climate.

In Chapters 3 and 4 we explore innovative ways in which different systems have sought to strengthen their services for children and their families. First we look at the development of knowledge frameworks and assessment models that articulate the knowledge base and we look at analytical decision-making processes that guide practitioners in their work. Whilst we only touch on a few of the innovative practice approaches that have been developed in recent years, we hope we have captured the key dimensions that strengthen practice overall: clearly articulated knowledge frameworks; engaging assessment models; and analytical decision-making processes that can be used in partnership with families.

Continuing the theme of partnership with families in Chapter 4 we explore family engagement strategies in child protection. Internationally systems have increasingly been adopting collaborative models of practice that harness the strengths of extended family to support children at risk. We look particularly at family group conferencing, a practice that recognizes the centrality of family in child protection decision-making. Now well embedded in some jurisdictions, the family group conference offers a way of moving from professionally-driven processes toward processes that are led by the families themselves.

Having examined the nature of child welfare practice and the ways in which the state responds to children at risk, the book then turns to the statutory systems of care for children. Over the past thirty years there have been tremendous changes in the way the state has provided care for children. In the first of three chapters dedicated to care Chapter 5 looks at kinship care, foster care, and residential care as key care types used when children cannot live at home. Depending upon the needs of the child, each care type can play an important role in providing out-of-home care. Chapter 6 discusses the providers of care, and the ways in which systems create positive out-of-home care environments for children. Rounding off the care chapters, Chapter 7 considers the experiences and voices of children who have been in out-of-home care. Given that systems of alternative care have far-reaching effects on the children that experience them, and that our best information about that experience is likely to come directly from them, it is critical that we listen to what children have to tell us about their experience, and then use these insights to inform the development of care services.

Child protection work operates within an uncertain environment where information is likely to be incomplete and there is often dispute over the facts. Sharpening critical reasoning skills and strengthening decision-making is important within this contested environment and as we draw the book to a close we return again to practice and consider ways of supporting good practice. We consider notions of practice depth, practice wisdom, and the complex dynamics that rest at the heart of child protection work. Creating opportunities for reflective practice and developing supervision processes that address key elements of child protection work is important to the strengthening of child protection practice. In Chapter 8 we develop five elements of safe practice that provide a foundation for a systems model of child protection supervision. We believe that investing effort in processes of reflective supervision has the potential to contribute significantly to the development of a stable workforce. Building a stable and experienced workforce is critical to the creation of strong and resilient practice systems.

Acknowledgements

As with projects of this kind, many people have contributed to the ideas contained within this book. Colleagues, students and practitioners who have shared their practice experiences with us have shaped our ideas about the ways in which practice is given effect in child protection. In particular we would like to thank staff within the Office of the Chief Social Worker in the Ministry of Social Development in New Zealand. Their high quality input has been greatly valued and we are grateful to them for their many insights and suggestions. We would also like to thank senior practice staff within the Department of Human Services, Victoria, Australia, for their helpful contribution to the workshop where we tested ideas relating to supervision and reflective practice.

We are grateful to our families, and in particular our partners George Hook and Bill Craddock. As always they have been enormously encouraging and tolerant, generously covering for us as we spent spare hours in front of our computers.

Finally we thank the University of Melbourne and the University of Nottingham for their ongoing support and the staff at Palgrave Macmillan for their enthusiasm and commitment to the project.

The authors and publishers are grateful to the following publishers and organisations for granting permission to reproduce copyright material in this book: Oxford University Press for Figure 3.2, originally from Connolly, M. (2007), 'Practice Frameworks: Conceptual Maps to Guide Interventions in Child Welfare', *British Journal of Social Work*, 37(5), pp. 825-837, Oxford: Oxford University Press; the Ministry of Social Development, New Zealand for Figure 3.7, originally from Weld, N. and Greening, M. (2004), 'The Three Houses', *Social Work Now*, 29 (December), pp. 34-37; the American Human Association for Figure 3.8, originally from Lohrbach, S. and Sawyer, R. (2004), 'Creating a Constructive Practice: Family and Professional Partnership in High-risk Child Protection Case Conferences', *Protecting Children*, 20 (2 and 3), pp. 78–92.

Every effort has been made to trace all the copyright holders but if any have been inadvertently overlooked the publishers will be pleased to make the necessary arrangements at the first opportunity.

Responding to children at risk

Key Points

- Views about children and childhood have changed over time, resulting in a greater emphasis on children's rights.
- Parents are expected to both nurture their children's development and well-being, and ensure that their children reach a level of healthy adult functioning where they can contribute to society.
- Increased understanding of the diverse needs of children and their families has resulted in countries exploring public health approaches to service delivery which includes an emphasis on primary prevention.

How often has one generation looked askance at the parenting of another? What a parent considers spirited behaviour in a child looks suspiciously like audacious defiance to a grandparent. Responsive child-rearing to one generation can look like chaotic mismanagement to another. These are changing attitudes played out in Western families as each generation works out what they think is the right way to bring up their children. Childhood and the relationship between children and the family have undergone major transformations over the past two hundred years. Changes in contemporary family life also result in changing views about the ways in which society can protect and care for children at risk. In this chapter we will explore these changes in attitudes, the impact of family adversity, and the ways in which society has sought to provide services that will support good outcomes for children.

Children and childhood

Concepts of children and childhood are culturally and socially defined. The management of children and the practice of childhood are buffeted and modified by demographic, political, economic, religious, and philosophical trends and debates (Baker, 2001; Harding, 1999). The history of childhood reveals changing patterns in the distinction between childhood and adulthood, the separation between the two being a fairly recent phenomenon (Baker, 2001; Harding, 1999; Knutsson, 1999).

The relationship between children and adults has also changed over time. Children were once viewed as 'property', where their well-being was the responsibility of their parents rather than society (Postman and others cited in Furman and Jackson, 2002). In the nineteenth century, however, particularly in the US, children of immigrants and the poor were removed from their parents when their well-being was considered to be at risk (Axinn et al. cited in Furman and Jackson, 2002). At that time, the prevalent focus was on the economic value of children in terms of their contribution to the family income; later, in the twentieth century, the focus was on the value of their emotional contribution to family life, in bringing 'love, companionship and enjoyment' to their parents (Cameron cited in Baker, 2001: p. 120). From being 'economically useful', the child has become 'economically useless' but 'emotionally priceless' (Hutchison and Charlesworth, 2000: p. 577). Childhood is viewed as a preparation for adulthood, with the family responsible for providing an environment within which the child can develop and grow (Furman and Jackson, 2002). And yet, even here, the economic value of children lingers in the subtle shift from the emphasis on the 'utility' of children to viewing them as 'a national resource or investment for the future' (Cameron cited in Baker, 2001: p. 120). Yet curiously, the emotional value of children is again captured as the dynamics between children and their parents take a further twist. With trends leaning toward transitional adult partnerships and the diversity of family structures, 'parent-child bonds are now often more enduring and less dispensable than partnerships' (Pryor and Rodgers, 2001: p. 1).

The separation of childhood from adulthood has led to the notion of children's rights as distinct from the rights of adults.

Children's rights

There are two theoretical positions – protectionist and liberationist – which explain this development (Baker, 2001). The protectionist view emerges from a traditional welfarist approach and focuses on the dependence and vulnerability of children. Their age and level of development renders them less capable of self-determination; consequently, adults make decisions for them while they are cared for in the context of the family with the support of the state. This is not the more recent liberationist view, which considers adult power and the emphasis on the family and the state as key providers of child care as oppressive. Rather, this approach focuses on the competence of children, 'with children's greatest need being for more power and autonomy' (Harding, 1999: p. 64). There are some obvious dangers in the liberationist approach, particularly in that children may be 'cast adrift' as the degree of parental and state responsibility for their care lessens. The liberationist approach has brought some advantages for children, however, with the recognition that children do have the ability to contribute to decisions that are made for them (Harding, 1999). This is a subject that we will return to in Chapters 4 and 7 when we look at the child's experience of statutory services and the increased expectations of participatory practice with children. Both the protectionist approach, with its emphasis on the welfare of children, and the liberationist approach, with its emphasis on empowering children, are evident in the Convention on the Rights of the Child (OHCHR, 1989; 2003).

According to the Convention on the Rights of the Child, childhood is a time when children are 'entitled to special care and assistance' within the context of the family, which in turn, should receive support and assistance from the community:

> (T)he family, as the fundamental group of society and the natural environment for the growth and well-being of all its members and particularly children, should be afforded the necessary protection and assistance so that it can fully assume its responsibilities within the community, ... the child, for the full and harmonious development of his or her personality, should grow up in a family environment, in an atmosphere of happiness, love and understanding, ... the child should be fully prepared to live an individual life in society .... (OHCHR, 2003: p. 1)

While the convention stipulates that the family is the ideal place for children to be nurtured, it also affirms the individual rights of children. Children's rights, as espoused by UNCROC, focus on three main areas: provision, protection, and participation. The right to provision relates to such things as family, health, and education. The right to protection relates to protection from discrimination, violence, and all types of abuse. The right to participation relates to such things as name, identity, consultation and freedom of speech. Summarizing the aims of the UNCROC, Knutsson (1999, p. 137) contends:

> The Convention has helped create a potentially new political situation in favour of children. It aims to alter perceptions about children and childhood and to foster the promotion of fundamental universal values in a world of far-reaching cultural, social, economic and political diversity. [...] The Convention ... represents a breakthrough in policymaking for the betterment of children. It indicates areas in which rights exist and should be protected and identifies goals and priorities for short- and long-term betterment strategies. Thus, the Convention stresses the continuum between child rights and child betterment.

The convention also has particular relevance to Indigenous communities. For example, provisions relate to: 'the right of children to preserve their own identity (Article 7) and the right of Indigenous children to enjoy their own culture, religion and language (Article 30)'. Furthermore, it encourages collective responsibility for children, representing values that resonate strongly with Indigenous communities. Concerns have been expressed at the Eurocentric concepts that idealize the individual and minimize collective practices, and challenges to their cultural fit have been raised (Ministry of Youth Affairs, 2000).

Whilst the issue of children's rights has moved to the forefront of public and professional concern in recent years, the overlapping needs and interests of children and their parents nevertheless create tensions, primarily played out within the family, but also critically impacting on the development of family social policy and the delivery of children's services (Connolly and Ward, 2008). Emerging within the context of family rights and responsibilities, this tension is crystallized in the debate relating to the corporal punishment of children.

Within this debate three positions have been identified: the pro-physical punishment lobby which is based in a firm conviction that it is a parent's duty to correct their children and support laws that allow them to do so; the 'conditional corporal punishment' (Taylor, 2005: p. 14) position which considers that the effects of punishment are not necessarily good or bad – physical punishment can have a positive impact in the context of a caring and nurturing environment; and the anti-physical punishment lobby which sees such punishment as an infringement of the child's human rights, which is degrading and inhumane (Taylor, 2005; Newall, 2005).

Whether parents have a right to physically punish children is a question that many countries have confronted. Twelve countries have fully abolished the corporal punishment of children: Sweden (1979), Finland (1983), Norway (1987), Austria (1989), Cyprus (1994), Latvia (1998), Denmark (explicitly in 1997), Croatia (1999), Germany (2000), Israel (2000), Iceland (2003) and New Zealand (2007); and others are considering whether reform is desirable (Connolly and Ward, 2008).

KEY PRACTICE QUESTIONS 1.1

1. How has the UNCROC created the possibility of what Knutsson describes as a new political situation favouring children?
2. How might tensions relating to family rights and responsibilities be played out in the home situation?
3. What issues might confront a country considering the abolition of the corporal punishment of children?

Child-rearing and parenthood

Characteristics of families, their structure, organization, roles and expectations, dynamics and expected lifestyles, differ across cultures (Pecora, Whittaker, Maluccio and Barth, 2000). Cultural values influence approaches to parenting, the ways in which children are supervised, parent/child relationships and the role of the extended family in the care of children, the ways in which children are supervised, and the division of parenting tasks and roles. In the context of cross-cultural perspectives, there is little agreement that any particular set of child-rearing standards have universal applicability (Connolly and Ward, 2008). Cultural knowledge and practices are passed down through generations of parenting, shaping beliefs and influencing behaviours over time. Responses considered abusive in one cultural environment may not be considered so in another (Fontes, 2005).

Increased diversity of family structure characterizes the modern family, with family members having responsibilities across households and generations. Blended families make family reunions larger and more complex, whilst changing demographics and kinship structures change the nature of familial relationships (Grundy and Henretta, 2006). The dichotomy that has separated parenting roles, allocating men to legal guardianship of children and women to the responsibility for child caring, has also undergone change. Yet as the structure of families devolves into a greater diversity of relationships, the role of the mother continues to be valued as the primary caregiver responsible for child-rearing (Hogget, 1993; Pryor and Rodgers, 2001). That said, as sole parent families become more common, opportunities for fathers to be involved with the day-to-day care of their children diminish. For children in divorced, separated, or sole parent families, the time spent with their fathers varies, with some children having no contact at all. Yet indications are that there are positive benefits for the well-being of children when fathers are motivated to spend time with them and provide them with care and nurturing (Kost, 2001; Pryor and Rodgers, 2001).

Dichotomous categories of 'good' and 'bad' parenting are based on social expectations of the ideal family; ideals, often based on myths, may not be attainable in reality (Munford and Sanders, 1999). Sole parents and those dependent on state income support, for example, tend to be judged as not fitting the 'norm'. Parenting difficulties are, however, contextual and are not of themselves an indicator of 'bad' parenting. What constitutes 'good' parenting centres around meeting the emotional and physical needs of children. Yet in an environment where economic disadvantage limits access to resources, parents can have difficulties in meeting their child's health and developmental needs.

Parents not only have a responsibility to attend to aspects of the developmental process that positively contribute to their children's well-being, they also have a responsibility to society to ensure that their children reach a level of healthy adult functioning where they can contribute to society. In order to achieve this, parents are responsible for ensuring the child's identity, safety, access to adequate medical care and education, and the development of appropriate behaviour patterns. The state is responsible for assisting parents by ensuring all children have access to publicly-funded and supported welfare, education, and medical services. The state also has a responsibility to set minimum standards for parenting, and to provide alternative care for children when these standards are not achieved and the child is at serious risk of harm (Hogget, 1993).

Children, families and adversity

Adversity has many faces, and while a single adverse event may have little impact in the long-term, the accumulation of harm can create ongoing problems for children in terms of their development and behaviour patterns (Smith, 1999; State of Victoria, 2007). The effects of adversity are particularly evident when there is an accumulation of negative experiences and circumstances. A number of stressors can affect children and their families, including poverty, parental conflict and violence, mental health issues, and parents' misuse of drugs and alcohol.

Poverty

Poverty has been identified as a contributing factor in the escalation of adverse family circumstances that can compromise the well-being of children (Berger, 2005). Low income over long periods is likely to have a negative effect on outcomes for children, with studies highlighting the effects of parental income throughout childhood into adulthood in terms of cognitive development, educational attainment, and finally employment and adult income levels. Research exploring the relationship between low income, contact with the benefit system, and children in sole parent families, indicates that, 'more than half of children born in the mid- to late-1990s may have been exposed to low income for at least part of their early years' (Ball and Wilson, 2002: p. 114). Clearly, financial factors alone may not affect the type of parenting children receive – other problems may also be implicated, such as psychological and physical health, low parental cognitive ability, and the parents' use of drugs and alcohol (Mayer, 2002). Nevertheless it needs to be acknowledged that these factors may also have their basis in low levels of income and indicate the cyclical impact of intergenerational poverty. Further, children from ethnic minority groups and sole parent families are particularly vulnerable to the health and developmental problems associated with poverty. Social isolation compounds the problem and is a contributing factor in child neglect.

Parental conflict and violence

The environment of care that children experience within the context of the family is provided predominantly by their parents, or parental figures. Few households are conflict free, and it is unlikely that children will entirely escape the experience of conflictual dynamics within the home. Increasingly, however, conflict results in the separation of parents, resulting in losses for the child associated with diminished contact or a lack of contact with the non-custodial parent. Research indicates, however, that:

> (C)hildren can survive and flourish after family change, when their parents are not isolated and unsupported, and can provide a warm, accepting but consistent and firm family environment. There are many examples of families who do cope and whose children are resilient and doing well. (Smith, 1999: p. 286)

Clearly, regardless of the circumstances preceding separation and divorce, children differ in their responses: 'some children suffer ... others recover and thrive' (Pryor and Rodgers, 2001: p. 3). Children do not always know why separation has occurred and may blame themselves. They may experience a raft of emotions: bewilderment, sadness, confusion, despair, anger, fear, and anxiety. Where a parent is absent, children may experience loss and abandonment, which can lead to feelings of rejection and low self-esteem. Where family dynamics have been typified by conflict and violence, children are often caught up in the paradox of feeling relief that the conflict is over, anger at the abusing parent, wanting the family to be reconciled, and longing to be with the absent parent.

Where children have witnessed parental violence, these repeated events can also compromise the child's emotional, cognitive and social development:

> Lack of critical early life nurturing, chaotic and cognitively impoverished environments, persisting fear and physical threat and, finally, watching the strongest most violent in the home get what he wants ... these [children] have been incubated in terror. (Perry, 1997: p. 10)

A number of factors have been identified that can ameliorate the impact of family violence on children including the parenting style, the degree of stress that the mother is exposed to, the child's gender, the child's relationship with the abuser, and the degree to which the child is resilient. Yet in situations of adult violence, helping services often overlook the needs of the child, and thus risk perpetuating the trauma rather than assisting children through the recovery process (McIntosh, 2002).

Parental mental health issues

According to Monds-Watson and her colleagues (2010) sixty per cent of women who experience ongoing mental health issues have children under 16 years. Most parents with mental health problems, however, look after their children effectively and well (Parrott et al., 2008). It is clear nevertheless that their vulnerability is high – they are more likely to experience unemployment and poverty, poor physical health, social isolation and stigma (Monds-Watson et al., 2010). Not surprisingly, these multiple stressors can impact on the vulnerability of children, and can be potentially exacerbated if they have less formal contact with school and their broader social network (Parrott et al., 2008).

In a summary of the research, Slack and Webber (2007) note the increased risk for children whose parent has a mental illness: parental negativity; family discord; attachment insecurity and parental affective style; ineffective discipline; and a child's future risk of an affective disorder. Because of the transactional nature of family life and parenting, the effect of parenting with mental health problems can clearly be an issue for children. In the context of child protection, the diagnostic condition of the parent is arguably less important than their behaviour toward the child and the child-rearing environment they provide (Monds-Watson et al., 2010). That children can experience distress in the context of maternal depression is more to do with the transitional impact it can have on attachments and the provision of care as opposed to the mother experiencing depression per se.

Although parenting in the context of mental illness presents challenges and can be unpredictable, there are nevertheless factors that build resilience for parents. Cultural strengths can support families, and parenting capacity can be enhanced in the context of 'satisfying employment, good physical health and professional, community and personal support' (Parrott et al., 2008: p. 1).

Parental misuse of drugs and alcohol

Parental misuse of drugs and alcohol can create an environment of potential harm for children. It can result in parents being physically and emotionally unavailable to their children, and increases the risk of child maltreatment and child welfare intervention (Jeffreys et al., 2006; Knoke, 2009). According to Jeffreys and her colleagues (2006: p. 3) 'drug and alcohol misuse is not a peripheral issue but a core component in a substantial majority of situations where children enter care'. Summarizing Knoke (2009: p. 1) parental misuse of drugs and alcohol can:

- Induce or increase negative feelings such as depression, anxiety or irritability;
- Interfere with the amount of control that the parent has over his or her emotional reactions;

- Impair a parent's mental functioning, problem solving and judgement;
- Interfere with parents' capacity to provide adequate care and supervision;
- Be associated with lifestyles that are harmful for children;
- Increase a family's stress in ways that tax a parent's abilities to cope effectively with child-rearing challenges.

When parents are not in control of their behaviour, children are inevitably at risk, and the younger the child the greater their vulnerability. If a parent is in a substance-altered state their capacity to make sure that their child is safe is likely to be compromised. Children can be exposed to abusive people, left unsupervised, or they could be physically hurt in a range of ways, for example, being laid upon by a parent in an alcohol-induced sleep. Precious family resources could be spent on satisfying their addiction resulting in the child being malnourished and neglected.

Working with drug and alcohol addiction in the context of child protection is one of the most difficult areas of practice where often families are struggling with a range of associated adversities that can include poverty, homelessness, violence and mental health problems. Taken together they create significant vulnerability for children:

> Substance abuse rarely occurs in isolation but typically coexists in combination with a constellation of issues which create high levels of risk to children.
> (Jeffreys et al., 2006, p. 4)

KEY PRACTICE QUESTIONS 1.2

1. What factors can negatively impact on a parent's ability to meet their child's health and developmental needs?
2. In what ways can the accumulation of harm create ongoing problems for children?
3. How might communities work to ameliorate key risk areas for children?

The maltreatment of children

Over the past twenty years there has been a series of child death reports that bring sharply into focus the vulnerability of children. We do not know how many children are abused and neglected, but we do know that it has been going on for a very long time. In the 1950s and 60s professionals became increasingly concerned about intergenerational neglect (Horwath, 2007). In 1962 Henry Kempe and his colleagues brought community and professional attention to the plight of physically abused children (Tomison, 2002). From that time, the *battered child syndrome* became a term used by professionals, and child physical abuse was projected into the spotlight. Once alerted to the issues children face, systems of welfare worked to develop their protection services for children. It was increasingly recognized that responding to child abuse required skilled intervention by trained professionals.

Over time, professionals became increasingly aware of child abuse and protection issues (figure 1.1). Women began talking about their experiences of childhood sexual abuse, and society began to take notice. A determined effort was made to seek more knowledge – people began to undertake research and write about this violent phenomenon that threatened the innocence and safety of children. While the sexual abuse of children had been an aspect of human history for generations, it did not fully become an issue of professional concern until the 1970s. As awareness grew, more complex understandings of the nature of adult offending began to emerge, as well as that of adolescent abusers and children who molest other children. In addition, the risk to children accessing the internet began to create concern. The prevalence of sexual exploitation of children through this medium has been raised as an increasingly serious problem, and from an Australian perspective Stanley (2001: p. 16) notes, 'given the dramatic growth in internet usage … it is imperative that safeguards be put in place now, rather than in a decade's time, when it may well be too late'. These issues stretched community and professional knowledge and expertise. Knowledge, however, evolved relatively slowly over time:

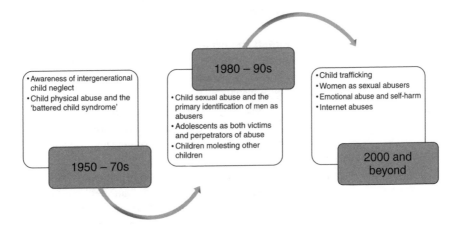

Figure 1.1 Developing knowledge of child maltreatment

In the context of contemporary practice, each area of child maltreatment presents challenges in definition, assessment and response. Legal definitions of abuse and neglect tend to be nominal definitions (Gelles, 1982). They are broad and guiding rather than specific. Legal definitions establish the parameters of abuse and are vague but flexible (Chan, Elliott, Chow and Thomas, 2002). In contrast to these nominal definitions, practice definitions are operational definitions, found in professional guidelines and protocols (Gelles, 1982). These are typically more detailed, for example as shown in table 1.1.

Table 1.1 Types of abuse (adapted from Fanslow, 2002)

Child physical abuse	Any act that may result in injuries being inflicted on a child or young person, including but not restricted to: bruises and welts; cuts and abrasions; fractures or sprains; abdominal injuries; head injuries; injuries to internal organs; strangulation or suffocation; poisoning; burns or scalds.
Child sexual abuse	Any act that results in the sexual exploitation of a child or young person, whether consensual or non-consensual, including but not restricted to: non-contact abuse; exhibitionism; voyeurism; suggestive behaviours or comments; exposure to pornographic material; contact abuse; touching breasts; genital/anal fondling; masturbation; oral sex; penetration of the anus or vagina; encouraging sexual acts; involvement in activities for the purposes of pornography or prostitution.
Child emotional abuse	Acts of omission resulting in impaired psychological, social, intellectual and/or emotional functioning and development of a child or young person, including but not restricted to: rejection, isolation or oppression; stimulation and affection deprivation; inappropriate expectations; inappropriate criticism, threats, humiliation, accusations; exposure to family violence; corruption (e.g. illegal or antisocial activities); impact of substance abuse or negative caregiver characteristics (e.g. emotional condition).
Child neglect	Acts or omissions that result in impaired physical functioning, injury and/or the impaired development of a child, including but not restricted to: physical neglect (failure to provide the necessities of life and health); neglectful supervision (failure to provide supervision leading to increased risk of harm); medical neglect (failure to seek, obtain or follow through with medical care); abandonment; refusal to assume parental responsibility.

While guidelines and protocols provide important information about risk decision-making in child welfare, in practice, much depends on the professional's own personal and professional judgement. Professionals bring their own beliefs about parenting, child care and abuse. Like everyone else, they are members of a socio-cultural environment, and this inevitably influences their professional decisions. According to Chan and her colleagues (2002: p. 363), this can have far-reaching consequences in terms of children's outcomes:

> (P)rofessionals' differing definitions of child abuse and child discipline
> have led to different intervention actions being taken in similar child abuse
> cases. ... They assess levels of abuse differently, make disparate decisions
> about placement or removal of the child from the home environment, and/or
> suggest dissimilar treatment programmes for the abusing adult or the abused
> child even when cases are similar.

Further complicating matters, some aspects of child abuse, emotional abuse in particular, are extremely difficult to assess. Styles of parenting differ, and it is difficult to draw an absolute line when it comes to acceptable and unacceptable psychological parenting (Corby, 1993). This has raised considerable debate and tensions in practice, particularly when working cross-culturally. Chan et al. (2002: p. 361) captures this tension nicely:

> Accepting claims of ethnocultural differences in raising children increases
> the possibility that corporal punishment of children by family members, for
> example, may be further legitimized. This may then prevent professionals
> from intervention in cases of abuse, resulting in them doing too little too
> late to protect children. ... Yet to dismiss cultural differences may result in
> professionals doing too much too soon, thereby irreparably harming families.

In addition to definitional and assessment complexities, each area of child maltreatment presents challenges with respect to response.

Child neglect

Parental neglect of a child usually reflects an ongoing or chronic lack of care that is often associated with cumulative developmental problems for the child (State of Victoria, 2007; Horwath, 2007). Neglect does not, however, appear in a single form. Carers can neglect children in a range of ways. *Physical neglect* is perhaps most familiar to practitioners (Horwath, 2007). In these situations the child lives in a poor and unhealthy living environment described vividly by Horwath, 2007: p. 33):

At its worst the smell of dirt, decay and excrement hits you as you enter the home. The floor is filthy and your shoes stick to the surface. There are children, dogs and cats everywhere. Clothes, stale food and the general detriment of daily living lie around you. There is little furniture and what is there is broken or damaged. [There is] evidence of damp and other health hazards in every room.

Responding to child physical neglect requires that the worker carefully assess the adequacy of the parenting environment and use their professional judgement to decide the nature and type of professional intervention required. Value judgements are made, and it is not unusual for workers who are continually confronted with the effects of poor physical environments to become desensitized to poor conditions and the impact these can have on the child.

A lack of adequate nutrition creates situations of *nutritional neglect*. In essence this is where a child does not receive enough nourishment to thrive and grow. In some situations this may result in what is called *failure to thrive*, where a child's growth is interrupted and they remain well below their expected milestones. In responding to suspected nutritional neglect it is essential that a good medical assessment is undertaken to ensure that there are no physical or medical barriers to the child developing as might be expected.

Failing to provide medical treatment for a child can have serious effects and is referred to as situations of *medical neglect*. Parents may not recognize their child's medical needs, or they may ignore problems. Sometimes a parent may hold religious beliefs that cause them to refuse treatment which is a difficult issue to deal with, particularly when the parents otherwise appear caring.

Parents may also provide inadequate supervision and guidance for their children. In these situations, children can find themselves in harm's way without a protective adult to look out for them. Being left home alone, or a child's experience of abandonment are good examples.

Neglect can have a damaging impact on a child's physical, emotional, cognitive and behavioural development (Horwath, 2007), and the more pervasive, the more harmful it becomes (State of Victoria, 2007).

The physical abuse of children

Although child neglect is generally the most frequently reported form of maltreatment, it is child physical abuse that creates community

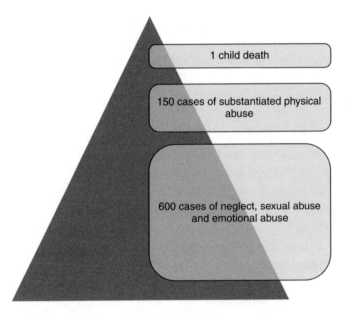

Figure 1.2 Australian estimates of abuse relative to one child death from maltreatment (adapted from UNICEF, 2003)

outrage, particularly when a child dies through homicide (Connolly and Doolan, 2007). The numbers of children who die from maltreatment represent the 'tip of the iceberg' of children who are maltreated, neglected or abused. UNICEF (2003)[1] reports an Australian study that found that for every child death from maltreatment there is likely to be on average 150 substantiated cases of physical abuse, and 600 cases if neglect, sexual and emotional abuse are included (see figure 1.2).

Exposure to child physical abuse, like child neglect, can have a significant impact on a child's healthy development, impairing physical and mental health, impacting negatively on psychosocial adjustment, cognitive ability, and the capacity for the child to form strong attachment bonds (Marie et al., 2009). Short-term physical effects of abuse may be relatively minor, for example, cuts and bruises. They can also, however, be severe, causing broken bones, internal bleeding, or death. Long-term consequences of babies being shaken have been

[1] Australian Institute of Health and Welfare, Child Protection Australia, 1999–00, Canberra 2001, cited in UNICEF, 2003.

identified as blindness, learning deficiencies, intellectual disability, cerebral palsy, and paralysis (Conway, 1998). Brain development can be negatively affected, and research has linked abuse with a range of poor health outcomes (NAIC, 2004). Summarizing the literature, NAIC report a number of psychological and behavioural consequences (table 1.2).

Assessing and responding to child physical abuse, whilst to the uninitiated may seem straightforward, is in fact an emotionally charged and highly complex endeavour. Indeed Munro (2002: p. 44) has argued that 'since risk assessment is, by definition, making judgements under conditions of uncertainty, there is an unavoidable chance of error. It is impossible to identify infallibly those children who are in serious danger of abuse'. This is an issue we will return to later in the chapter.

The sexual abuse of children

Since the increased awareness of the prevalence of child sexual assault within society, considerable attention has been paid to the potential effects of childhood sexual abuse on the developing adult. Research into the consequences of child sexual abuse has been wide-ranging, and findings have indicated significant negative outcomes for victims of abuse. This has included an association with a range of mental health problems: 'depression, anxiety, anti-social behaviours, substance use,

Table 1.2 Consequences of abuse (adapted from NAIC, 2005)

Psychological Consequences	Behavioural Consequences
Poor mental and emotional health: • depression, anxiety, eating disorders, suicide attempts, panic disorders, dissociative disorders, attention-deficit/hyperactivity disorders, post traumatic stress disorder Cognitive difficulties: • language delays • lower cognitive capacity • lower academic achievement Social difficulties: • poor attachment patterns • relationship difficulties with adults and peers	Difficulties during adolescence: • delinquency, teen pregnancy, low academic achievement, drug use, mental health problems Juvenile delinquency and adult criminality: • increased likelihood of arrest • increased likelihood of adult criminal behaviour Alcohol and other drug abuse: • increased likelihood of smoking • increased likelihood of alcohol and drug abuse • abusive behaviour towards others

suicidality, and other psychiatric problems' (Fergusson et al., 2008: p. 608). A history of child sexual abuse has also been associated with other adult concerns including problems with communication (Blum and Gray, 1987), behavioural problems and antisocial conduct (Watkins and Bentovim, 1992; Luntz and Widom, 1994).

Over time, knowledge regarding the perpetration of child sexual abuse has expanded to include men and women who sexually offend, a growing appreciation of adolescent sexual offending, and sexually aggressive children. Each of these areas now has a well developed body of knowledge that seeks to better understand the sexual exploitation of children (in particular see: Hunter, 2006; Woodiwiss, 2009; and in the context of disability, Higgins and Swain, 2010).

Behavioural issues and child welfare

Although services for children at risk are most commonly associated with responding to child abuse and neglect, they also respond to childhood conduct and behavioural problems. Managing difficult behaviour can cause immense difficulties in family life, and there is a significant body of research that explores disruptive and antisocial behaviours in childhood and adolescence (Utting et al., 2007; Tremblay et al., 2008). Conduct problems can disrupt home and school life and when overstepping legal boundaries can draw children, young people and their families into criminal justice systems.

In general children show signs of physical aggression early, but then it diminishes as the child grows and gains new skills that help them manage their emotions. According to Tremblay et al., (2008: p. 8):

> About five to 10% of children maintain highly aggressive behaviours as they grow out of their preschool years. Children who do not learn from an early age to replace their physical aggression with more socially appropriate behaviours, such as communicating verbally, compromising and cooperating with others, are at a considerably increased risk for school troubles and school drop-out, delinquent and criminal behaviours, substance abuse problems and unemployment.

Services are provided to children and families across the family life-course. The more entrenched the behaviours become, the more difficult it is to find solutions that positively support the retention of children and young people within their family system.

KEY PRACTICE QUESTIONS 1.3

1. How might service responses to neglectful parenting differ from child physical abuse interventions?
2. How might difficulties in defining the abuse and neglect of children create problems from a service intervention perspective?
3. How might insights into the effects of childhood abuse and neglect assist workers assessing childhood behavioural problems? How might they also create misleading assumptions?

Good outcomes: well-being, attachment and resilience

Good outcomes for children are measured in terms of their social and intellectual competence, and their physical and psychological well-being. Good outcomes are achieved through positive parenting, a stable family life, strong family and kin relationships, community involvement, and supportive social networks. As Bronfenbrenner (cited in Knutsson, 1999: p. 130) puts it:

> The effective functioning of child-rearing processes in the family and other child settings requires public policies and practices that provide place, time, stability, status, recognition, belief systems, customs and actions in support of child-rearing activities not only on the part of parents, caregivers, teachers and other professional personnel, but also relatives, friends, neighbours, co-workers, communities and major economic, social and political institutions of the entire society.

Interest in good outcomes for children has led to studies that have explored the correlation between attachment patterns, emotional and behavioural attributes, and the development of resilience in children as indicators of their well-being.

Well-being

Well-being is defined in terms of the ability of families to access emotional and material resources within the social and economic environment (Munford and Sanders, 1999). Family well-being depends on the capacity to care for children and fulfil their basic developmental, health, educational, social, cultural, spiritual, and physical needs; children's well-being depends not only on having their basic needs met but also on having 'the opportunity to grow and develop in an environment that provides consistent nurture, support and stimulation' (Pecora et al., 2000: p. 5). The nurture of children is the central function of most families, where 'warm and reciprocal affective relationships' allow children 'to progress from dependence to independence' (Smith, 1999: pp. 268–69). In other words, for children to grow and thrive in the world they need love, protection, support and the opportunities that will help them develop the skills they need to succeed. Sadly, the close-knit communities that once provided families with mutual support and assistance in their child-rearing roles rarely exist (Smith, 1996). More and more the state is required to develop formal methods of providing families with the support communities were once able to offer.

Attachment

The early years of a child's life, long recognized as the most formative, are also years when the child develops secure attachments that will strengthen his or her ability to cope with adversity.

> There is no doubt that children's experiences in the early childhood and
> primary years have a lasting effect on their development. The first 6 or
> 7 years of life are fundamentally what determines the kind of people we
> become. (Smith, 1996: p. 6)

Attachment between the child and the primary caregiver is pivotal to the developmental process. Among other things, secure attachment is linked to intellectual and language development, exploratory and socially appropriate behaviour, autonomy rather than dependence and the ability to form relationships, and can serve as a 'buffer against stress'; the securely attached child will have a positive relationship with the parent, while the parent is less likely 'to act in ways that are detrimental to them' (Atwool, 1997: pp. 158–60).

Children also have the ability to form multiple attachments, and this serves them well when alternative forms of care are needed. For children who have experienced abuse or neglect, however, their ability to become securely attached to a caregiver may be disrupted or compromised. Studies reveal that this group of children risks developing a range of maladaptive and antisocial behaviour patterns. Thus they may have difficulty in forming relationships, have poor problem solving and coping skills, and may be prone to aggressive and violent behaviour (Finzi et al., 2001; Lawson, 2001; Robinson, 2002).

Resilience

The notion of resilience shifts the perspective from viewing children as 'at risk', to acknowledging their capacity for 'resilience' in overcoming the effects of adversity. It is closely associated with the concept of attachment:

> It is clear that resilience is not an isolated individual characteristic [nevertheless it] is difficult to see how … protective factors could be acquired outside the context of secure and consistent attachment. (Atwool, 2007)

Positive parenting, along with protective factors based on family cohesion, belief systems, coping strategies, and communication skills contribute to the development of resilience, while the adverse effects of risks, such as single parenthood, teenage parenting and poverty, can be mediated by the parenting behaviour and how the family copes when managing on few resources (Mackay, 2003). Other factors associated with positive parenting include participating, being involved and having 'high expectations' of children (Bernard cited in Johnson, Howard and Dryden, 1997).

Resilience may not necessarily be a 'discrete quality' (Johnson et al., 1997: p. 168) but may fluctuate across the lifespan depending on circumstances (Atwool, 2007). Nevertheless, intervening early provides an opportunity to provide support before problems become entrenched. The arrival of a new baby, for example, provides a 'window of opportunity' (Atwool, 2007: p. 17) to work with parents to improve the quality and strength of attachment bonds.

Developing services for children at risk

Creating positive outcomes for children is a shared responsibility. Parents, families and communities provide care and nurturing for children. But it is clear that whilst the majority of children are cared for well, there are some that are subjected to abuse and a lack of care. This is where community and professional services play a role in supporting good outcomes for children, and state systems provide the safety net for those children most at risk. Yet many writers have noted the increased intensity of child protection and family welfare work over the past thirty years (Birmingham, Berry and Bussey, 1996; Briar-Lawson, Schmid and Harris, 1997; Pecora, Whittaker and Maliuccio, 1992) arguing that, internationally, child protection systems have experienced a multi-dimensional crisis (Barter, 2001; Scott, 2006). A dramatic rise in the number of children reported to authorities in English speaking jurisdictions has raised significant issues with respect to how services will cope with increased expectations that they will take responsibility for all concerns relating to the care and protection of children (Connolly and Doolan, 2007).

The pressure from this increased demand is evident across international jurisdictions. In the US during the fiscal year 2007 child protection services received an estimated 3.2 million referrals of suspected child maltreatment (5.8 million children), approximately a quarter of which were substantiated as abuse (US Dept of Health and Human Services, 2007). In England social workers receiving and investigating concerns of child abuse and neglect have experienced a rise in the numbers of cases referred for attention since 2007. Research undertaken by the Association of Directors of Children's Services, revealed that safeguarding activity by social workers had increased by an average of 21 per cent in two years (ADCS, 2010).

Australia and New Zealand have also seen a continued rise in the number of notifications of concern for children considered to be at risk. In Australia from 2004/5 to 2007/8, notifications increased by 26 per cent to 317,526 (Australian Institute of Family Studies, 2009). Substantiated abuse increased from 46,154 in 2004/5 to 55,120 in 2007/8, and children on care and protection orders rose by more than 100 per cent, from 16,449 in 1998 to 34,279 in 2008. In New Zealand notifications have increased from 25.4 per 1,000 children in 1997 to 96.4 per 1,000 children in 2008. Indigenous children in both Australia and New Zealand continue to be overrepresented in the numbers of children receiving statutory services and care.

Over two decades, a complex set of drivers, including this increase in demand, shaped the way in which contemporary services have been provided for children at risk. High profile cases in the media have placed child protection at the forefront of public concern, and a new managerialism reinforcing the bureaucratization of child protection have been instrumental in reducing responsiveness to children and families (Ferguson, 2004; Munro, 2011). Response became increasingly forensic and uniform – a 'one-size-fits-all' protection response to children at risk (Munro, 2002; Scott, 2006). Screening the population for at risk children, undertaking more and more child abuse investigations and destabilizing families, writers argued, had the potential to actually *increase* the risk of child abuse for many children (Scott, 2006). As a consequence Western systems have developed 'like a giant Casualty Department required to respond to a flood of patients, the vast majority of whom do not require hospitalisation and would be much better managed by the local GP' (Scott, 2006: p. 6). So what might the equivalent of the local GP look like in the context of child welfare service delivery? In part, the answer lies in the research relating to *early intervention*.

Increasingly, research indicates that intervening early in the life of a child or a problem brings the best long-term results (Scott, 2009; Wiggins et al., 2007; Bannon and Carter, 2003). Early intervention helps children do better socially and educationally, improves health and well-being, and has the potential to reduce violence with the family over the long-term by providing support for new parents that is focused on prevention:

> There is widespread consensus that the best way to protect children is to prevent child abuse and neglect from happening in the first place. There is also widespread consensus that this requires robust primary and secondary systems for protecting children that provides families with the assistance they need before they come into contact with the statutory child protection system. (Allen Consulting Group, 2008: p. 3)

Moving away from the ambulance at the bottom of the cliff response that has typified child protection services' responses in recent decades, a *public health* approach supports the building of preventative solutions that have the potential to reduce the accumulation of risk factors over time. Most families need support at one time or another. Many families call upon their own resources at these times, or seek to access universal services that are designed to respond to the adverse challenges that modern families face. Some families, however, remain isolated and struggle to manage alone. Increasingly service systems are refocusing their responses to include an emphasis on early intervention (Axford and Little, 2006). In a public health approach an emphasis on primary prevention has been integrated with targeted and tertiary responses across the sector (figure 1.3) as a way of strengthening whole-of-system of service responses.

KEY PRACTICE QUESTIONS 1.4

1. How might risk-averse child protection responses impact on the delivery of services for children and families?
2. What impact might the development of a public health model have on service delivery?
3. What are the strengths and weaknesses of the primary, targeted and tertiary services within your locality?

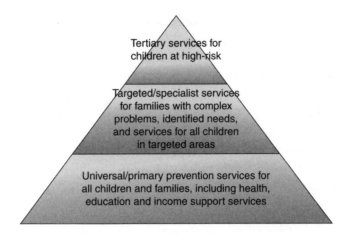

Figure 1.3 Integrated service system reflecting a public health model of service delivery

Yet, early intervention as a strategy for supporting families has also been the subject of critical analysis, particularly with respect to the privacy implications of monitoring a whole population in order to identify children at risk (Parton, 2006; Munro, 2007; Munro and Parton, 2007). These are issues of significance moving forward:

> The relationship between human rights, early intervention, and the perceived
> need for public surveillance mechanisms to further preventative aims is a
> complex one. It is, however, one that is likely to rest at the heart of
> future human rights debate as human services seek to take advantage of
> developments in technology and governments seek to balance meeting the
> interests/needs of individuals with addressing the broader interests and
> concerns of society. (Connolly and Ward, 2008: p. 181)

Conclusion

Family structures continue to adapt and evolve new forms within the social, economic and political environment of the Western world. Cultures influencing each other have introduced conflicting attitudes towards standards and expectations regarding the relationship between parents and their children. While the UNCROC has highlighted a number of issues that affect the health and well-being of children, countries bring their own perspective to these. Across the globe, in terms of health, education, and well-being, children of disadvantaged cultural groups are frequently over-represented in welfare statistics. Nevertheless, how well families are able to provide for children depends on a number of factors. These include supportive family relations and social networks, and access to social capital and economic security. Within this context, children are able to develop secure attachment patterns, which, in turn, can provide the basis for building resilience or the capacity to cope with adverse circumstances. Despite experiences of conflict, trauma and deprivation, good outcomes can be achieved. This knowledge can provide hope and instill confidence that children who have suffered abuse and neglect can be nurtured and supported through their pain and their struggles in their journey towards well-being and independence.

In recent years child welfare systems have explored ways in which services can be provided to address diverse family needs. This has included developing alternatives to the one-size-fits-all statutory child protection service response. We will now look at some of the different ways in which countries have approached the care and protection of children, and will consider the development of service models that increase the range of service responses.

FURTHER READING

Arney, F. and Scott, D. (2010) *Working with Vulnerable Families: A Partnership Approach*, New York: Cambridge University Press.

Howe, D. (2005) *Child Abuse and Neglect: Attachment, Development and Intervention*, Basingstoke: Palgrave.

Parton, N. (2006) *Safeguarding Childhood: Early Intervention and Surveillance in a Late Modern Society*, Basingstoke: Palgrave.

USEFUL WEBSITES

The National Child Protection Clearinghouse, accessible at: http://www.aifs.gov.au/nch/

The New Zealand Child, Youth and Family website, accessible at: http://www.practicecentre.cyf.govt.nz

United Nations Human Rights: Office of the Human Rights Commissioner, accessible at: www.ohchr.org/EN/Pages/WelcomePage.aspx

2

Regulatory frameworks in child welfare

Key Points

- Countries have developed different approaches to child welfare, both with respect to overall service orientation and to the ways in which they intervene in the life of a family.
- Many countries have developed alternative or differential responses to service delivery that provide more attuned responses to family need.
- Child protection services are constantly evolving, developing within a dynamic and often politically charged environment.

A key aim of a child welfare system is to influence the ways in which parents raise their children. Statutory systems have formal powers within law to protect children and are therefore considered to be 'highly formalized regulatory systems' (Braithwaite et al., 2009: p. 5). In fact, regulation of human activity occurs across a spectrum from the least formal, for example, families regulating actions in and around the home – to highly formal regulatory processes when governments impose rules upon citizens. A range of regulatory systems exist across the primary, secondary and tertiary sectors in child welfare, all of which can play a role in keeping children safe. In the care and protection of children, who intervenes in the life of a family, and when they intervene, are essentially questions of regulatory intervention. When the state receives a report of concern for a child, determining levels of regulatory intervention inevitably presents complex dilemmas, particularly in the context of increased negative media exposure and growing expectations that services will never fail a child at risk.

There is no question that during the decade of the 1990s child welfare systems across English speaking jurisdictions were exposed to intense pressure in the delivery of child care and protection services.

As we noted in Chapter 1, heightened awareness of child abuse has resulted in greater numbers of children being referred to child protection services, in turn placing considerable pressure upon the responsive capacity of statutory systems. It is nevertheless clear that not all families who are notified to statutory services need to be subjected to a full child protection investigation. Indeed, it is unnecessarily intrusive to require a full investigation and it is more likely to result in an adversarial or hostile response. Providing more responsive regulatory frameworks across a spectrum of services that can make a difference for children and their families has therefore become a key priority for child welfare systems in recent years. In this chapter we will look at the ways in which different jurisdictions have developed systems of response, the orientations that have influenced their service delivery, and some of the challenges in finding the right regulatory system in some of the more complex areas of child and family welfare practice.

Creating responsive regulatory frameworks

Countries have their own ways of defining abuse and neglect, and they have their own ways of responding to family issues. Systems develop in response to a unique set of social and cultural conditions, and because of this, services, policies and practices can vary considerably across international jurisdictions. Countries have been found to differ both in their broad philosophy and orientation to child welfare, and the way in which they manage notifications of child abuse and neglect.

According to Hetherington (2002), three important factors influence the development of child welfare systems: structures, professional ideology, and culture. Structural systems provide the mechanisms through which services are delivered. These may be organized at a central governmental level, or they may be provided by local non-government systems. The structural system influences both the way in which interventions occur, and the thinking behind them. For example, Grevot (2002: p. 3) argues that the French child welfare system:

> ... is rooted in the spirit of the Fifth Republic, with the symbolic alliance between the State and the family for the up-bringing and education of children – child being understood both as a member of a family as well as a citizen to be.

The development of the children's judges system as the 'secular arm of the state' created the structural framework that would influence the French system of child welfare for fifty years. It gives the French system a unique flavour around which services for families have developed. How services fit together is also important. In the UK, the call for a 'whole-of-government' approach, providing more integrated systems of welfare, health, and education, if successful, will influence the ways in which cross-sectoral relationships develop and are sustained in that country.

Legal frameworks contribute importantly to the structural system. How the law provides for the needs of children and families in child welfare clearly influences the way in which practice is undertaken. Recourse to the court system represents the highest level of regulatory activity where statutory powers to remove children from their families may be used to keep children safe. Writers have begun to challenge the appropriateness of legal action and interpretations dominating practice (Sheehan, 2009; Harlow, 2003; Preston-Shoot et al., 2001). Fundamental tensions exist for practitioners attempting to support families and negotiate their way through complex child protection matters in the context of increased accountability expectations. Exploring the negative aspects of this tension, Braye and Preston-Shoot (2002) argue:

> This emphasis on legalism is problematic. Essentially, this is because legalism conflates good practice with 'procedurally correct' practice, the latter emphasizing apparent certainties rather than acknowledging the imprecision and choice points inherent in social work tasks. ...The statutory mandate is neither consistent nor comprehensive; it is confused and ambiguous.

To combat this, Sheehan (2009) maintains that workers need to adhere to a 'best practice' position and be able to recognize when the law can inadvertently divert practice from this:

> Developing a practice framework that positions a legal perspective within an overarching set of integrated practice perspectives, including principles-based best practice, research evidence, clinical knowledge and practice wisdom, will provide greater confidence that we are striking an appropriate balance and practice in the best interests of the people we are working with. (Sheehan, 2009: p. 340)

The law, of course, can also create a context for alternative regulatory processes. For example, the introduction of the Children, Young

Persons and Their Families Act [CYP&F Act] (1989) in Aotearoa New Zealand[1] radically changed the way in which children and families are responded to, and has set the standard with respect to participatory practice with families in child care and protection. The introduction of the Family Group Conference (see Chapter 4) legally set in place a process within which extended families could 'self-regulate' by coming together and making decisions about the care of their children. The Children's Act (1989) in the UK has also been significant in laying a foundation for the flourishing of partnership practice with families.

How systems of welfare develop is also influenced by professional ideology. Social workers have theories that guide their practice and influence their decision-making in child care and protection. For example, in the past two decades, models of best practice in child welfare have reflected greater commitment to family empowerment and family participation in processes that concern them. In this way practitioners have sought alternatives to legal solutions within the highly regulated child protection system. Significant developments have been the family preservation and reunification movement, widely adopted in the US to address the permanency issues for children and the exigency of the growth in foster care (Connolly, 1999). The competence-centred perspective, which represented a shift from more traditional pathology or deficit models has also been influential (Pecora et al., 1992), and so, too, the more recently developed strengths-based perspective that harnesses the strengths of the family and its network toward the protection of the child. According to Hetherington (2002), while organizational structures, resources, and law provide the framework for child welfare practice, actual decision-making is often based on professional knowledge and theory. Systems that allow greater use of professional judgement will look different from highly bureaucratized systems with heavily proceduralized requirements.

Finally, Hetherington talks about the way in which regulatory frameworks are influenced by the culture of the society within which they exist: 'Culture influences and expresses expectations of the various roles that should be played by the state, the family, and by the community in relation to the child' (Hetherington, 2002: p. 14). Since child welfare encapsulates the complex relationships between state and

---

1 Throughout this book, the terms Aotearoa, Aotearoa New Zealand and New Zealand are used interchangeably to refer to the country of New Zealand and its territories.

family, it is significant that the ways in which a society perceives these relationships influences both philosophy and practice. Because culture can be constantly changing, yet at the same time resistant to change (Hetherington, 2002), its impact on the development of systems of response in child welfare cannot be underestimated.

KEY PRACTICE QUESTIONS 2.1

1. In what ways can cultures within a society influence the development of regulatory frameworks in child welfare?
2. What might a legalistically dominated child protection practice system look like?
3. How might professional ideology influence service development across the regulatory spectrum?

Orientations to child welfare

Although there would appear to be considerable commonality in terms of the challenges facing child protection systems internationally, writers have nevertheless identified differences in the way in which countries have developed their service responses. Spratt (2001), for example, notes a basic 'schism' reflecting opposing positions in child welfare – one that characterizes a family support orientation, and one that characterizes a child protection orientation. The *child protection orientation*, representing a highly formal regulatory framework, is characterized by:

> ... a primary concern to protect children from abuse, usually from parents who are often considered morally flawed and legally culpable. The social work processes associated with this orientation are built around legislative and investigatory concerns, with the relationship between social workers and parents often becoming adversarial in nature. (Spratt, 2001: p. 934)

By comparison, the *family support* orientation has been characterized as having 'a tendency to understand acts, or circumstances, thought of as harmful to children, in the contexts of psychological or social difficulties experienced by families' (ibid). Here, families are seen as needing support to enable them to undertake the task of parenthood, and services are provided to ensure that they have the best possible chance of successfully looking after their children.

Relevant to this is Gilbert's (1997) comparison of child protection systems in nine Western countries. Gilbert argued that it is possible to differentiate child welfare responses into these two welfare orientations: child protection and family service. Countries that have a 'child protection' focus, such as, England, Canada and North America, he found to be more legalistic in approach, delaying intervention, and applying resources at the investigative 'front-end' of the child protection process. Alternatively European countries, such as Germany, Denmark, Sweden, Finland, the Netherlands and Belgium, were found to have a 'family service' orientation. These countries place a much greater emphasis on prevention and the provision of less formal early support services. Although these distinctions are necessarily generalized and to a degree oversimplified, they do provide a context for understanding the ways in which regulatory frameworks have developed over time. More recently, along a similar vein, writers have explored differences between Australian/American/UK responses on the one hand, and Continental West European approaches on the other (see Table 2.1).

Understanding the orientation of service delivery is important because it impacts on the degree of formality that a system provides in the delivery of social services. Developments in Australia have generally paralleled those in the US, Canada and the UK, with an emphasis on risk assessment and the application of resources at the investigative process level. Hetherington (2002) notes that the English speaking

Table 2.1 Child welfare orientation (adapted from Hill, Stafford and Lister, 2002: p.6)

Characterized by child protection systems in North America, UK, and Australia, reflecting:	Characterized by child protection systems in Continental West Europe (Belgium, Sweden, France, Germany) reflecting:
• a tendency toward residual and selective provision of welfare • child protection services being separated from family support services • a more legalistic, bureaucratic, investigative, adversarial response to child protection • emphasis on children's rights and child protection • emphasis on investigating risk • concentrating state resources on families identified as immediate and high-risk	• a tendency toward universal welfare provision • child protection services embedded within broader family support orientation • a voluntary, flexible, solution-focused, collaborative approach to child protection • emphasis on family unity and a systems approach to family • emphasis on support and therapeutic assistance • resources available on basis of early intervention

countries, such as England, Scotland, Northern Ireland, Ireland and Australia, were generally child protection focused and crisis orientated in their research, reflecting a legalistic approach that is distrustful of less authoritative intervention. By comparison, child welfare systems in France, Germany and Sweden, having developed more slowly, are embedded within a broader system of universal welfare and have a greater emphasis on informal systems of family support and mediation. Because they are built on a foundation of universal welfare provision, they have been found to engender community support which is less obvious in the more adversarial, legalistic systems described above. These services are described as strengths-based, working 'in solidarity with parents, as part of a well developed system of social welfare offered as a right, voluntarily, and, with resources to support families' (Hill et al., 2002: p. 8).

KEY PRACTICE QUESTIONS 2.2

1. In what ways does a child protection approach differ from a family support response and what tensions may exist between the two orientations?
2. What might the challenges be in either orientation?
3. What orientation best characterizes the child welfare system in your locality?

Over time, the increased emphasis on child safety and a lower tolerance for conditions that are considered abusive have contributed to a more 'interventionist' approach in child welfare (Farris-Manning and Zandstra, 2003) and writers have argued the need to reclaim a 'family-centred services reform agenda' (Mannes, 2001: p. 336). The cultural shift toward forensic responses is nevertheless strongly embedded in practice and inevitably has a significant impact on the ways in which child abuse and neglect notifications are managed. Challenged by these issues, countries are exploring their regulatory systems across the spectrum of services so that more responsive interventions can be provided for families.

Finding the right regulatory response

International research has suggested that the majority of welfare needs are ignored in the process of child abuse and neglect investigations (Thorpe and Bilson, 1998), and it is clear that an increasingly narrow forensic response to the investigation of child safety has been at the expense of providing broader family support services (Scott, 2006;

Buckley, 2000; Sandau-Beckler, Salcido, Beckler, Mannes and Beck, 2002; Spratt, 2001). Child protection work that is driven by administrative requirements, strict procedures, and the primacy of management over professional practice has been described as the 'bureaucratization' of child protection (Tomison, 2004). In many systems of child welfare, despite families often presenting with more generic problems, this 'forensically-driven' child protection system has resulted in all families being responded to as 'high-risk' and, therefore, being exposed to a full child protection investigation (Scott, 2006; Tomison, 2002). Hence, families have been subjected to a 'one-size-fits-all' response (Rogers, 2003; Scott, 2006; Lonne et al., 2009) regardless of need. Writers have argued that more intensive family-focused services have the potential to increase practice depth and the opportunities for workers to both protect the child and support the family (Cameron and Vanderwoerd, 1997). Given the concern to address both the lack of service depth and responsiveness to diverse family needs, it is perhaps not surprising that many countries have explored ways in which the dual mandate to support the family and protect the child can be accommodated within an integrated family-centred response. Differential response models, also referred to as alternative stream/track models, which are now functioning across a range of jurisdictions, have been introduced primarily to address the limitations of the 'one-size-fits-all' response. They are designed to be more flexible and engaging, and to better understand the issues underlying child maltreatment reports (Child Welfare Information Gateway, 2008). Driven by a desire to move from a solely investigative response, child welfare systems have looked to differential response as a way of increasing their responsiveness to the needs of the family. Simply put, families that need a statutory response receive one, and families that are assessed to need more general family support services receive an alternative response more appropriate to their needs.

Family support services as early interventions can detect children at risk before they reach the statutory threshold for protective intervention (Tomison, 1995). The forensic style child protection is a highly intrusive intervention that has the potential to militate against the engagement of low-risk families. If a family presents as needing support rather than requiring an investigation of abuse, engaging them in a voluntary process and building a positive casework relationship is likely to be more effective. Family engagement and involvement in the process of the work is essential to collaborative problem solving. Family investment in the process of the work is more likely to result in a greater family commitment to the outcome (Connolly, 1999). Risking the loss of engagement with families through an unnecessary investigative process may reduce the potential for families to be active (and willing) participants in the change process. Hence, providing an alternative supportive service response is likely to enhance the potential to engage families on a voluntary basis. This is particularly important in cases of child neglect where working in partnership has considerable benefits:

> Involvement of parents in assessment, decision-making, treatment, or interaction is essential to make things work, even if the child has to be removed from home. ... The point is that without parental agreement and commitment to work towards mutually recognised goals, progress is not going to be made at home. (Iwaniec, 1996: p. 121)

In addition, neglectful parenting situations generally require longer-term support services. Because of this, the shorter-term services offered by child protection systems tend to be less successful.

At the resourcing level, a consequence of the 'one-size-fits-all' response is that limited resources tend to be expended at the highest regulatory level. The effort needed to undertake a full investigation of all notifications has often meant that lower-risk notifications have had to wait for service, being left unattended and assigned to waiting lists. Many countries have found that as low-risk families remain unsupported their situation exacerbates and they return as higher-risk cases. Important opportunities are therefore lost for secondary prevention work. In addition, according to Whittaker and Maluccio (2002), the 'one-size-fits-all' approach does not respond well to families whose needs change over time. These demands make it difficult to provide effective and timely responses to families across the risk continuum.

How differential response systems work
Many countries that reflect a child protection orientation have reformed their systems to incorporate elements of a differential or alternative response. The practice is widespread in the US, and similar developments can be found in Canada, Australia and New Zealand. While the alternative response systems reflect the particular country's unique service network and language relating to the systems may differ, in

general, they follow a similar structural pattern: following a report of concern (or notification), an assessment is undertaken to distinguish whether the situation requires a child protection or family support response. If a family support service is required, then this will either be provided by a team within the statutory agency, or, more typically, the family will be referred to a non-government family support agency. Figure 3.1 captures the essential elements in a differential response system.

Although a family may be referred for a family support response, if it is later considered that a child protection response is more appropriate, then the child would be referred across. Equally, if the initial assessment indicates a child protection response, but further enquiry reveals that a family support response is required, then the family would be provided with the more appropriate service. The emphasis is on flexibility. Although practices in the UK do not necessarily identify as a *differential response* system, a comprehensive assessment framework is used to ascertain the type of service required (see Chapter 3). The assessment framework explores a number of dimensions to provide a systematic approach to analysing information about children and families. The dimensions relate to the child's developmental needs and well-being, the ability of caregivers to respond to those needs, and the impact of external factors on the parent's abilities (Department of Health, 2000). Overall, guidelines strongly support inter-agency assessment of children at risk arguing that voluntary and private organizations can provide important

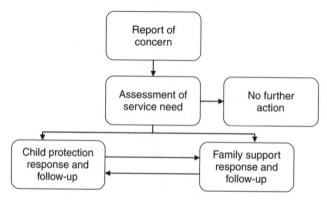

Figure 2.1   A model of a differential or alternative response system

to act in situations where risk to children is ambiguous (Connolly, 2009). The involvement of statutory child protection when a child is exposed to witnessing domestic violence in the home has resulted in the issue being framed as one of child protection. This analysis was supported by research, particularly in the 1980s and 90s, suggesting it was harmful for children to be exposed to violence in this way (see for example, Appel and Holden, 1998; Fantuzzo and Lindquist, 1989; Groves, 1999; Jaffe et al., 1986). Child protection services responded, as one might expect, using a child protection regulatory intervention, investigating the risk to children and considering the impact of witnessing violence on the well-being of the child. In framing the child's exposure to domestic violence in child protection terms, any further intervention is then based on risk to the child and the parent's capacity to protect.

Given the well developed arguments supporting responsiveness to service user need, the questions we must ask in these situations is whether a child protection intervention is justified, and secondly is it the right regulatory framework to use? Exposure to domestic violence may be harmful, but is it necessarily child maltreatment? This question was challenged in Minnesota when state legislature changed the definition of child neglect to include a child's exposure to domestic violence (Edleson et al., 2006). Although seen as a modest change in the law it did, in fact, unleash a set of unintended consequences as statutory child protection services were quickly overwhelmed with reports of children witnessing domestic violence. Reframed as an issue of child neglect, protective services put pressure on abused women to leave the violent home situation – to remain within the home demonstrated a lack of protective parenting and therefore neglect of the children. Not surprisingly, advocacy services for battered women in Minnesota expressed considerable concern about this shift toward 'woman-blaming', and worked with the Minnesota child protection services (who also had misgivings about the change) to successfully repeal the law in 2000. A child protection statutory intervention was no longer justified and according to Edelson et al. (2006: p. 172) 'Minnesota no longer considers children exposed to adult domestic violence to be neglected'. The state of Minnesota is not unusual in having reframed a child's witnessing of domestic violence as a type of child maltreatment, although arguably it went further than most other jurisdictions in legally defining it as such. Many Western child protection systems continue to receive referrals for children exposed to domestic violence and continue to reframe the issue as one of child protection.

This logically takes us to the second question: does the child protection approach provide the most appropriate regulatory framework? If the problem is essentially one of interpersonal violence, it could be argued that a child protection intervention package is unlikely to be the most useful in facilitating change within the family system. A child protection regulatory intervention generally assesses a child's exposure to domestic violence on the basis of seriousness of risk. Its focus is on parenting rather than reducing harm within the couple relationship. A solution from the perspective of the child protection service is to encourage the woman to distance herself from her abusive partner. Yet these expectations may lack synergy with the needs and experiences of the people involved (Friend et al., 2008). For a variety of reasons, the woman may not want to leave the home. She may be concerned about the potential for heightened risk if she tries to leave. Or there may be religious or cultural barriers that make such decisions more complex. Despite the abuse, she may continue to value the relationship and the unity of the family.

Providing a regulatory response that is out of sync with the needs and concerns of the family is unlikely to support good long-term solutions. Situations of low-risk family violence are unlikely to demand authoritative child protection action and in the absence of remedial service support may result in multiple referrals to child protection services and multiple investigations with similar outcomes. In situations of more serious family violence where an authoritative child protection intervention *does* occur the solutions may be equally out of sync and may even have the potential to make things worse instead of better.

If the argument for alternative responses to domestic violence cases involving children is accepted, an important next question is: who across the regulatory framework is better able to provide it? Shlonsky and his colleagues (2007) argue that after 30 years of providing services in the context of domestic violence we may be at the point of challenging some fundamental issues relating to the responsiveness of family violence interventions. As we have said, many women are unable or unwilling to leave abusive partners, and for these women the provision of safe house facilities is not necessarily a solution or appreciated. Frustratingly for workers, even when women do leave violent situations, it is not unusual for them to go back, or find themselves in other relationships that are equally abusive while their abusive partners go on to abuse other women and children. This creates a serial domestic violence cycle that is all too familiar to professionals working in the fields of child protection and family violence.

These situations of intimate partner violence where risk to children is ambiguous provide a good example of the need to think carefully about both the level and nature of the regulatory framework that is most likely to respond to the needs and aspirations of the service user, and therefore create more potential for positive change. It is clear that domestic violence referrals to statutory child protection services often create a mismatch with respect to the presenting issues and service responses. Whilst undoubtedly the right response for some women, the provision of support and safe housing through traditional domestic violence services may also represent a mismatch for others. Looking across the service spectrum and extending alternative responses, where appropriate, becomes imperative. Staffed by professionals familiar with complex family violence dynamics and skilled in addressing risk factors associated with domestic violence (for example, issues of mental health, and drug and alcohol misuse, Mackness, 2008), whilst interfacing closely with services for women, men and children, has the potential to provide increased options for couples wanting to stay together. Shlonsky et al. (2007: p. 359) refers to this type of service as one of *harm reduction* in couple relationships, giving people a chance to live together safely and ultimately creating 'a coordinated, cross-sector effort to work with families ... (to) help our clients be informed consumers and to determine, to the greatest extent possible, the course of their lives'. In exploring alternative responses in the area of domestic violence it is important that a child's protective needs do not fall between the cracks of service delivery silos.

There are many challenges in developing regulatory processes that are responsive to children and families. Creating more robust ways of differentiating levels of risk will provide greater clarity regarding the type of service most suited to the child's needs. Whilst differentiating risk will never be an exact science, the better we are in linking needs and services, the better positioned the service community will be to respond. Any moves toward the development of a family-focused service would need to ensure that we do not return to times past when children's needs were not adequately recognized in the context of domestic violence situations. Rather, the service community needs to be integrated in ways that support the ongoing interests and aspirations of the people receiving the service.

KEY PRACTICE QUESTIONS 2.4

1. How might the aims of a child protection response differ from a service response in domestic violence?
2. What are the issues in providing a 'harm reduction' regulatory response in domestic violence when children are involved, and how can the needs of the child remain a priority?

Reforming child welfare

Child protection services are constantly evolving, existing within a dynamic and often politically charged climate. It is within this quickly changing environment that strategic planning and the management of child welfare reform takes place. At a time when most child welfare systems are undergoing reform it is important to consider the ways in which changes impact on practice in the longer-term, sometimes with unintended consequences. For example, much has been written about the 'bureaucratization' of child protection (Tomison, 2004) and the adverse effects of some managerial practices on the development of child protection systems (Munro, 2011; Lonne et al., 2009; Beddoe and Maidment, 2009). A lack of directional vision and clearly articulated principles to guide intervention pathways can result in child welfare practices being negatively influenced by waves of critical attack and 'scandal politics' (Ferguson, 2004). An important role of child welfare senior management is to provide a clear vision and a confident articulation of the logic behind the system's regulatory framework together with an integrated set of responses that are consistent with that vision and logic (Lonne et al., 2009; Connolly and Smith, 2010).

Statutory child welfare systems across the globe have risen to these challenges exploring ways in which their services can become 'less vulnerable to … outbreaks of moral panic and to consequent knee-jerk policy formulation, which have serviced to both inflate child-protection bureaucracies and subject their operation to yo-yo practice' (Spratt, 2008: p. 422). In the UK *The Protection of Children in England* action plan (HM Government, 2009) outlines the government's strategic direction aimed at strengthening services for children and families. This report sought to reinforce the arrangements necessary locally and nationally to address multi-agency practice and policy in safeguarding children. New layers of administrative arrangements were developed but this sat within a critical backdrop that argued for less rather than more bureaucracy (Munro, 2002). The extent to which protocols and process could enhance practice was debated and the new UK coalition government moved quickly to review this area. During their first weeks in office they introduced a review of child protection arrangements. Led by Professor Munro from the London School of Economics, the review was to seek ways of reducing unhelpful administration and supporting better practice (DfE, 2010). The Munro review (2010; 2011) has now been completed and its far-reaching recommendations have the potential to significantly influence the ways in which child protection is practised and supported in England.

Phase one of the Munro review identified four key drivers that have been influential in shaping the child protection system in England (Munro, 2011: p. 6):

- The importance of the safety and welfare of children and young people and the understandable strong reaction when a child is killed or seriously harmed;
- A commonly held belief that the complexity and associated uncertainty of the child protection work can be eradicated;
- A readiness, in high profile public inquiries into the death of a child, to focus on professional error without looking deeply enough into its causes; and
- The undue importance given to performance indicators and targets which provide only part of the picture of practice, and which have skewed attention to process over the quality and effectiveness of given help.

The review argues that these drivers have created a system that is defensive and highly proceduralized, shifting emphasis and staff effort toward meeting administrative demands over and above direct work with children and their families. The review's recommendations set out to address the unintended consequences of these drivers, to strengthen practice expertise, and to create a broader context that is supportive of effective social work practice. Briefly, recommendations across five broad areas include:

- *Developing a system that values professional expertise*
  Revising policies to clarify essential expectations and to develop a greater context for professional judgement-making; to reduce the current highly prescriptive approach to enhance opportunities for innovation; to create a more child-centred approach to the inspection framework; and to benchmark local authority performance based transparently on improvement and accountability.
- *Improving learning and clarifying accountabilities*
  Strengthening reporting lines; amending statutory guidance to take fuller account of local need; assessing the effectiveness of services and training; refocusing key senior staff on services for children; investment in research; and requiring the use of a systems methodology when undertaking serious case reviews.
- *Shared responsibility for early helping services*
  Increasing responsibilities for the provision of early helping services including the identification of services that are available, developing ways of identifying children at risk, resourcing early help services; and in situations where a child and family may not meet the criteria for children's social care services, to facilitate an 'early help offer'.
- *Developing social work expertise*
  The incorporation of child and family social work capabilities within the Professional Capabilities Framework which explicitly informs social work training and performance appraisals; that employers and educators work together to better prepare students for the challenges of child protection work. This includes the strengthening of quality placement opportunities.
- *The organizational context*
  Using an evidence and effectiveness framework, agencies begin an ongoing process of service delivery review and redesign; that Principal Child and Family Social Workers be appointed in each local authority to provide practice leadership; and the creation of a Chief Social Worker position to advise government on matters relating to social work practice.

These broad-ranging recommendations provide an important platform for change with respect to policy, practice and strategic reform.

Australia and New Zealand have also moved forward with respect to strategic reform. The national framework for protecting Australia's children (Council of Australian Governments, 2009: p. 7) has set the direction for service delivery that supports a *public health* model:

Australia needs to move from seeing 'protecting children' merely as a response to abuse and neglect to one of promoting the safety and wellbeing of children. ... Under a public health model, priority is placed on having universal supports available for all families (for example, health and education). More intensive (secondary) prevention interventions are provided to those families that need additional assistance with a focus on early intervention. Tertiary child protection services are a last resort, and the least desirable option for families and governments.

Having both a federal and state system of government, the national framework seeks to build a 'shared agenda for change' (p. 9), that recognizes the contribution of all levels of government with respect to the care and protection of children. Its aim is to provide leadership in the delivery of more integrated responses across the system, harnessing the strengths and resources at all levels. Its implementation plan (see Council of Australian Governments, 2009 for a full discussion of the reform agenda) describes action across the range of national priorities:

1. *Joining up service delivery,* focused specifically on the need to support a 'joined-up' approach to service design, planning and delivery, targeting particularly the most disadvantaged families.
2. *Closing the gaps,* by supporting Indigenous communities to protect their children in culturally responsive ways.
3. *Seeing early warning signs and taking early action,* by strengthening responses to at risk children through the provision of tools and resources that will improve early identification, assessment and joined-up working across the sectors.
4. *Improve support for carers,* by improving support for kin and non-kin carers.
5. *Developing national standards for out-of-home care,* to improve the care experience and outcomes for children who are not able to live within their own families.
6. *Building capacity and expertise,* by strengthening the education, professional development and retention of professionals across the sector, focusing particularly on Indigenous workforce development and expanding the range of professional contribution.
7. *Enhancing the evidence base,* including improvements in data collection and national reporting.
8. *Filling the research gaps,* by developing a national research agenda to inform future policy and service delivery.

9. *Transitioning to independence*, focused on providing greater support for children and young people leaving statutory care systems.
10. *Responding to sexual abuse*, undertaking research to better understand the challenges in providing a strong policy and service delivery platform.
11. *Advocating nationally for children and young people*, and exploring the potential appointment of a national Commissioner for Children and Young People.
12. *Sharing information*, and creating policies and processes that enable appropriate sharing of information across the levels of service delivery.

The national framework presents a set of opportunities for reform that have the potential to impact on the care and protection of children and the support of families across Australia. In a similar way, reforms in New Zealand have sought to strengthen the regulatory frameworks supporting children at risk. Whilst many systems undertake reform following a critical review, the New Zealand reforms emerged from an internal belief in the need for change, an internal analysis of the issues confronting the organization and the development of an integrated plan to address them (see Connolly and Smith, 2010 for a detailed description of the reforms in New Zealand). Identifying the strategic vision and a simple set of key priorities was the first step in the process of addressing the complex issues that confronted the service system. The priorities were based primarily upon the ways in which the service system could make a difference for children and their families. The strategic document *Leading for Outcomes* (Child, Youth and Family, 2007) provided the vision and a brief account of the following key priorities:

1. *Quality social work practice*, ensuring the highest standards of professional activity.
2. *Addressing youth offending*, creating a context within which young people can be supported to turn their lives around.
3. *Achieving permanency for children*, creating systems that support a context of belonging for children.
4. *Responding to community needs and expectations*, by working with communities to shape solutions that achieve lasting outcomes.
5. *Outcome focused residential facilities*, that are strengthened to provide intensive and creative responses for children and young people at highest risk.

6. *Leadership*, in supporting staff to step up and make a difference in their communities.

In the context of the first priority, *quality social work practice*, a set of professional reforms supported the strategic direction. An integrated model provided the conceptual plan that brought together four inter-related elements to support professional reform:

- A *knowledge framework* that provides a succinct picture of good practice that is both ethically- and evidence-informed (see Chapter 3).
- A differential response *service model* providing the pathway system supporting service responsiveness to families.
- The *practice package* providing the tools and resources that give effect to the framework and the service model, and
- A *staff support* strategy, which includes strengthening competency and promoting professional development, that would create an environment in which staff could do their best work.

According to Lonne and his colleagues (2009), reforming child welfare takes time, and there are inevitably challenges along the way that can threaten to derail the processes of change. It is clear, however, that systems continue to explore ways in which they can protect children while at the same time protect systems from 'knee-jerk policy formu-lation…(and) yo-yo practices' (Spratt, 2008: p. 422), and the child protection/family support pendulum swings that so often undermine services for children and their families.

Conclusion

Whilst it is clear that systems of child welfare across international jurisdictions have been confronted by enormous challenges, particu-larly over the past two decades, it is also clear that there have been significant efforts to strengthen the regulatory frameworks supporting children at risk. Broadening the scope of service delivery to include interventions across the service sector has been critical in the devel-opment of differential responses and most systems have indicated a strong commitment to strengthening services across the primary, secondary and tertiary systems. The complexity of contemporary issues will nevertheless continue to vex service delivery and will challenge systems to develop increased clarity regarding the nature and type of service that would be most likely to provide positive outcomes for children.

Strong regulatory frameworks in child and family welfare provide a means through which services can be clear about their mandate and creative in their service delivery. This includes creating practice environments that are supported by strong principles and evidence, international examples of which we now explore in Chapter 3.

FURTHER READING

Commonwealth of Australia (2009) *Protecting Australia's Children is Everyone's Business, National Framework for Protecting Australia's Children, 2009–2020,* available from http://www.coag.gov.au/coag_meeting_outcomes/2009-04-30/docs/child_protection_framework.pdf, retrieved 28 May 2009.

Lonne, R., Parton, N., Thomson, J. and Harries, M. (2009) *Reforming Child Protection,* London: Routledge.

Munro, E. (2011) *The Munro Review of Child Protection: Final Report. A Child-centred System,* available from www.education.gov.uk/publications/eOrderingDownload/Cm%208062.pdf.

USEFUL WEBSITES

The American Humane Association also provides excellent information on differential response and other areas of child welfare. It can be accessed at http://www.americanhumane.org/children/programs/differential-response/.

The Child Welfare Information Gateway is an excellent resource for information on differential response. It can be accessed at http://www.childwelfare.gov/pubs/issue_briefs/differential_response/differential_response.pdf.

3

Practice frameworks, models and resources in child welfare

Key Points

- Practice in child and family welfare evolves over time. Frameworks, models and tools giving effect to good practice need to be responsive to cultural imperatives, underpinned by strong ethical values and informed by quality research.
- Interventions reflecting a commitment to partnership with families are increasingly seen as good practice in child and family welfare.
- Robust child protection systems are supported by a clearly articulated knowledge base, sound assessment models that engage families, and effective professional decision-making processes.

Just as international jurisdictions create culturally responsive service systems to support their work with children and families, over time practice models have also been shaped by cultural imperatives, increased knowledge relating to what works, and evolving ideas about what represents good practice. It is clearly beyond the scope of any one book to incorporate all the new and good ideas that have informed child welfare practice across international systems. So in this chapter we decided to take an integrated approach by including a set of key ideas, drawn from international jurisdictions, and developed to increase our focus on good practice. We will start at the highest level of abstraction and describe the way in which research, ethical values and best practice ideas have been brought together in the development of *practice frameworks* in child welfare (Connolly, 2007). Frameworks provide a scaffolding of ideas that provide a logical and integrated explanation of a whole. We will argue that a clearly articulated picture representing a vision of practice has the potential to positively influence and strengthen the development of models, tools and resources that are consistent with good practice.

We will then look at the gathering of information in the context of a child protection enquiry, describing two assessment models: the *Assessment Framework* developed in the United Kingdom (Department of Health, 2000); and the *Best Interests Case Practice Model* developed in Victoria, Australia (Victorian State Government, 2008). Each provide similar, but uniquely different ways of exploring strengths, risks and the service needs of children and their families. Potentially augmenting more formal assessment models, we also describe *The Three Houses* (Weld and Greening, 2004), a simple but effective tool we think has the potential to enhance practice, particularly in the context of working with children.

Finally, we look at a process that helps practitioners to make sense of the information they have gathered throughout the process of a child protection assessment and strengthen the decision-making as they move forward. Here we draw upon the work of Turnell and Edwards (1999) and their *signs of safety* approach. The approach is, in fact, a partnership approach to practice that facilitates an engaging assessment with families, and provides a means through which information can be used to inform decisions moving forward.

In bringing these ideas, frameworks and models together we are not necessarily proposing that they be used as an integrated package, although some systems have done so (see for example, Connolly and Smith, 2010). Rather, we use them to illustrate what we consider to be three critical components in the development of robust practice systems: knowledge-based frameworks that articulate an ethical, evidence-informed vision for practice; engaging assessment models that address strengths, needs and risks; and analytical decision-making processes that can be used in partnership with families (figure 3.1).

Knowledge frameworks for ethical practice

Practice frameworks that articulate the child welfare knowledge-base and guide practitioners in their work have been developed in recent years to strengthen the knowledge/practice nexus in child welfare (Connolly, 2007), youth justice (Doolan, 2009) and criminal justice (Ward and Connolly, 2008). A practice framework:

> ...integrates empirical research, practice theories, ethical principles and experiential knowledge in a compact and convenient format that helps

practitioners to use the knowledge and principles to inform their every-day work. (Connolly and Healy, 2009: p. 32)

Much has been written about the issues in using empirical research to inform practice (Gray et al., 2009). Whilst some writers argue strongly for the singular importance of evidence-based practice (Yegidis and Weinbach, 2006), others maintain the importance of multiple sources of knowledge (Beddoe and Maidment, 2009). Lonne and his colleagues (2009) for example argue persuasively that there is a need to develop ethical frameworks that can help workers navigate their way through the murky relational dimensions of practice. We are persuaded by the latter, believing that frameworks based on research findings, ethical principles, natural justice and human rights, will help to clarify and reinforce practice behaviours that support good outcomes for children and their families.

An example of the development of a child welfare knowledge framework that was implemented to revitalize family practice can be found in Aotearoa New Zealand. The Care and Protection Practice Framework (Connolly, 2007), introduced in 2005, supports three

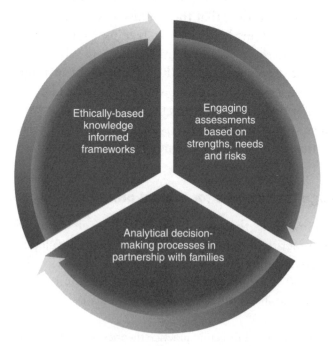

Figure 3.1 Critical components in the development of robust practice

key practice imperatives: child safety, family support; and family participation in practice. It identifies three key perspectives upon which practice is based: the child-centred perspective, family-led and culturally responsive perspective, and the strengths and evidence-based perspective, and arrives at a set of practice triggers, or best practice reminders, that are drawn from the research and practice literature across these three perspectives. The practice triggers are the mechanisms through which the practice framework translates research knowledge and good practice principles into action and weaves the messages from the literature through the phases of the work with families: engagement and assessment; seeking solutions; and securing safety and belonging for children. The metaphor used to describe the interwoven nature of the framework is a Māori *kete*, representing in this context a basket of knowledge (figure 3.2). The strands of practice are woven together, interrelating with each other and making a stronger whole. In this sense, one strand is not

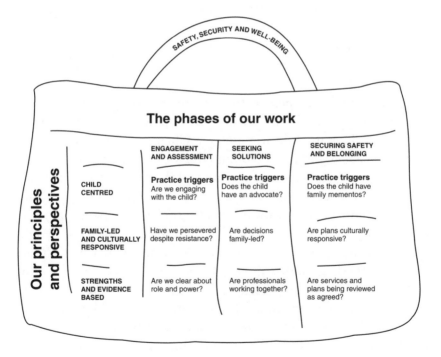

Figure 3.2 The New Zealand Care and Protection Practice Framework (Connolly, 2007). Reproduced with kind permission of the *British Journal of Social Work*.

enough – it is the weaving of the strands that makes the practice strong.

The framework's knowledge base

The *child-centred perspective* within the framework is supported by research and best practice literature focusing on the interests of the child (Connolly, 2007). Based on the principles of the Convention for the Rights of the Child (United Nations, 2006), the welfare and interests of the child are paramount and children have a right to preserve their own identity, to enjoy their own culture, religion and language. The framework is cognisant of the importance of listening to children and having them participate in decisions that affect them (Littlechild, 2000; Holland and O'Neill, 2006). In eliciting children's views directly adults show respect for children as persons (Morrow, 2004). Attachment theory and its application in the context of child abuse and neglect, is central within the framework. Stability of care and attachment has been found to be of critical importance to child well-being (Watson, 2005; Atwool, 2007) and the need to interlink the fields of attachment and child protection has been identified (Bacon and Richardson, 2001; Atwool, 2005; Mennen and O'Keefe, 2005).

In the same way the child-centred perspective is supported by research and best practice literature, so too is the *family-led and culturally responsive perspective*. A growing body of international research supports family engagement practices and family-led decision-making in child welfare (see Chapter 4 for a fuller discussion). Engaging family, including the extended family, has been critical in supporting the safe retention of the child within the kinship network and several studies have reported increased rates of relative care for children at risk (Edwards et al., 2007; Gunderson et al., 2003; Koch et al., 2006; Morris, 2007; Titcomb and LeCroy, 2003; Walker, 2005). Greater placement stability has been noted when children remain with their family group (Gunderson et al., 2003; Pennell and Burford, 2000) and shorter periods of time in care for children (Wheeler and Johnson, 2003). Importantly, increased kin support for the family has also been identified (Kiely and Bussey, 2001; Morris, 2007), with Horowitz (2008) finding increased emotional support (75 per cent), increased help with transportation (44 per cent) and increased respite care for the family (35 per cent). Building on the family's cultural strengths is also a key component of the practice framework. The quality of an individual's support network can impact on professional effectiveness (Sprenkle et al., 1999) and McKeown (2000) strongly argues a case for strengthening the informal supports that surround a family.

The third perspective within the framework relates to *strengths and evidence-based practice*. Understanding 'what works' in practice has the capacity to strengthen a practitioner's effectiveness (Trotter, 2004) and increase their skill repertoire. Good outcomes are achieved in a practice context of role clarity, the reinforcement of pro-social values, collaborative problem solving and good relationship work with a supportive helping alliance (Trotter, 2004). McKeown (2000) also reinforces the importance of the helping alliance noting that as much as 30 per cent of good outcomes can be directly attributed to the relationship between the worker and the family. In essence, this research reflects a strengths approach to practice supporting the notion that practitioners can support the development of resilience in family groups:

> ... resilience involves struggling well, effectively working through and learning from adversity, and integrating the experience into the fabric of individual and shared life passage. (Walsh, 2008: p. 6)

Turning knowledge into action: the framework's practice triggers

Once the knowledge base was identified and interrogated, key messages from the literature were translated into practice triggers – 'good practice' reminders that can trace their origin back to the research and practice literature. Child-centred practice triggers were developed, followed by practice triggers supporting the family-led and culturally responsive perspective, and the strengths and evidence-based perspective within the framework. The idea behind the framework is that the practice triggers are then woven together through the care and protection phases of the work: engagement and assessment; seeking solutions; and securing safety and belonging.

The *engagement and assessment* phase of the work begins with a report of concern for a child's care or safety and generally corresponds to the investigative phase in many systems of child welfare. The practice triggers provide reminders that we are being child-centred, family-led and culturally responsive, and strengths and evidence-based (figure 3.3).

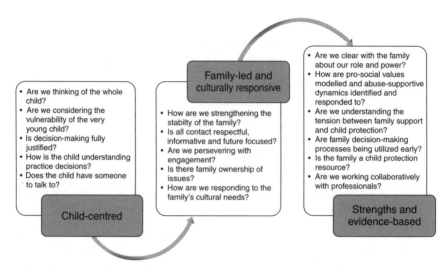

Figure 3.3 The 'engagement and assessment' practice triggers

The *seeking solutions* phase of the work begins once the worker's assessment identifies a child protection concern and work needs to be done to develop a solution. Within Aotearoa New Zealand this typically involves bringing together family, including extended family, in a solution-focused forum (the family group conference – see Chapter 4). Again, the practice triggers provide reminders for practice (figure 3.4).

Once plans are developed, work commences toward *ensuring safety and belonging* for the child. This phase of the work may involve support for the family with the child remaining at home, or it may involve a change of caregiver for the child, either with family or with alternative caregivers.

Hence, the practice triggers within the framework provide challenges to practice – reminders that reinforce and balance the perspectives throughout the phases of the work. They do not function as a checklist. Rather, they infuse a particular flavour into practice, encouraging critical reflection in practice and supervision. In this sense, they provide opportunities for practice dialogue. They frame practice understandings, and our collective beliefs around what is important to the work.

In essence, the practice framework articulates ethically-informed practice that supports strong engagement with families, harnesses the strengths of the child's extended family system, and reinforces longer-term safety and security for the child. From a practitioner's perspective it values professional practice and connects staff with the evidence

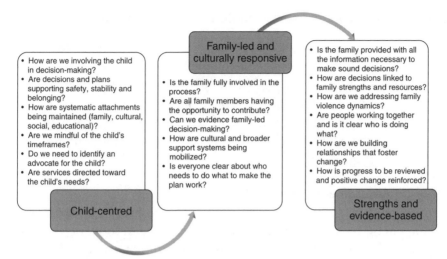

Figure 3.4 The 'seeking solutions' practice triggers

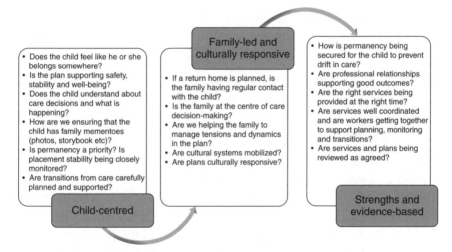

Figure 3.5 The 'securing safety and belonging' practice triggers

base that builds professional confidence. Perhaps most importantly, it sets a bar for practice delivery within the child welfare system providing a high level vision of practice that the service wishes to achieve.

KEY PRACTICE QUESTIONS 3.1

1. What are the benefits of having a high level knowledge framework to guide practice in child welfare and what challenges might they present?
2. Why are ethical principles important in child welfare work?
3. What contribution to practice can empirical research provide?
4. How might cultural imperatives be incorporated in frameworks for practice?

Developing assessment models in child protection

The second area considered critical in the establishment of a strong practice system is the development of engaging assessment models that address strengths, needs and risks. The UK assessment framework, which has now been adapted across international jurisdictions, is a good example of a systematic approach to the gathering of information in the context of a statutory child abuse and neglect enquiry.

The UK Assessment Framework

Introduced in 2000, the assessment framework represented a key component in an ambitious and wide-ranging reform of the UK system of child welfare. Overall, reforms promote more joined-up services, a more stable and skilled workforce to deal with the contemporary issues, and an environment within which information could be shared with respect to children at risk. In the context of strengthening practice the assessment framework was developed to provide:

> ... a systematic way of analysing, understanding and recording what is happening to children and young people within their families and the wider context of the community in which they live. (Department of Health, 2000)[1]

There are a number of principles upon which the framework is based. Firstly, assessments are fundamentally *child-centred*. At all times throughout the assessment process workers are expected to maintain a keen focus on the child, and consider carefully the child's perspective. This is to avoid the child's interests being lost in the context of complex, and often dominating, family issues such as housing problems, or family relationship conflicts. Assessments are also expected to be *rooted in child development*. Assessments need to be cognizant of a child's complex developmental needs and milestones, and interventions need to consider carefully the child's timeframes. Six months tend to pass like a flash for busy child welfare workers, but may nevertheless represent half a lifetime for a toddler in need of care and

1 For a full discussion of the UK assessment framework see Department of Health, 2000 (retrievable from http://www.dh.gov.uk/prod_consum_dh/groups/dh_digitalassets/@dh/@en/documents/digitalasset/dh_4014430.pdf).

protection. An *ecological approach* underpins assessments within the model. Understanding the child's needs and concerns in the context of the broader family, community and cultural network is important, and so too the influence of positive and negative environmental factors. It is this notion of an ecological approach that has shaped the domains of enquiry within the assessment framework which focus specifically on the child's development needs, the caregiver's capacity, and the wider family and environmental factors.

The principle of *equal opportunity* also underpins the framework, recognizing the importance of non-discriminatory practice and the need to ensure that systems do not reinforce or enhance discriminatory experiences. Inherent in this approach is the need to support individual and family potential and to respond sensitively to diverse cultural family contexts. Building *cooperative working relationships* with children and their families is also important within the framework, together with the need to *build on strengths* as well as recognizing the presenting difficulties within the family situation. Assessments are expected to be *inter-agency focused* as workers apply collaborative effort in the delivery of services to children and their families.

Understanding the issues confronting a family as a *continuing process rather than as a single event* reinforces the iterative nature of the assessment framework. More in-depth understandings that consider historical issues and the complex reality of the family's experience are more likely to result in considered and helpful responses. Assessments are also carried out in *parallel with other actions* and are considered to be an integrated part of a process of engagement and intervention with a family. Finally, the principle of assessments being *grounded in evidence* is supported, and the need to utilize multiple sources of knowledge to positively strengthen practice.

The assessment framework itself, influenced by an ecological approach, identifies three exploratory domains: the child's development needs; parenting capacity; and external family and environmental factors (figure 3.6).

Each domain has a number of dimensions that are all explored during the process of an assessment. In the context of a child's developmental needs, a child's *health* is an important consideration – is the child growing as expected? Does the child have a nutritious diet? Are the usual developmental checks undertaken (e.g. immunizations, dental and eye care etc)? The *educational* dimension covers the areas

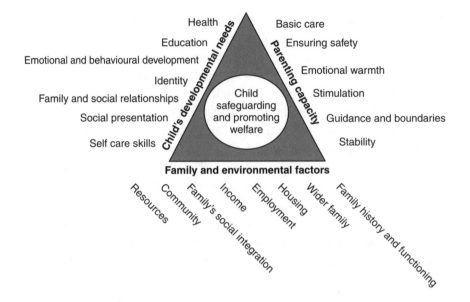

Figure 3.6 The UK Assessment Framework (Department of Health, 2000: p. 17)

of the child's cognitive development, including opportunities for play, learning and interaction with other children. The child's *emotional and behavioural development* is explored including the quality of attachment bonds, responses to stress and indications of resilience. The *identity* dimension relates to the child's growing sense of self, feelings of belonging and broader acceptance as a valued person in their own right. *Family and social relationships* are considered both with respect to the quality of relationships and their endurance over time. The child's *social presentation* and *self care* represent the final dimensions within the domain focusing specifically upon the way in which the child presents to the world, and their developing competencies and social problem solving abilities.

The parenting capacity domain within the assessment framework also has a set of dimensions for exploration. The parent's ability to provide *basic care* is considered including their responsiveness to the child's physical needs. Their demonstrated ability to *ensure safety* for the child provides a good indication of the parent's protective capacity, and their *emotional warmth* provides a context for the child to develop in the context of stable, secure and affectionate relationships. Fostering positive learning and *stimulation* indicates a parent's capacity to create a context of intellectual development for the child, whilst a parent's capacity to demonstrate positive *guidance and boundaries,* models positive values and social behaviour. Finally, a parent's capacity to provide *stability* enables a child to develop secure attachments and thus optimal development.

The third domain relating to family and environmental factors explores the *family history and functioning,* including their ability to overcome challenges, and considers the strengths within the *wider family.* Practical issues such as housing, employment and income are explored, including the ways in which these may impact on the relational issues within the family. Consideration is also given to the *family's social integration,* the strengths of their social networks, or conversely their level of isolation. The *community resources* dimension refers to the accessibility of services and facilities that the family could utilize, and the family's responsiveness to broader systems of community support.

The assessment framework has been a central component of the UK child protection approach for a decade, providing 'a conceptual map for gathering and analysing information about all children and their families' (Department of Health, 2000: p. 17). Whilst the recent Munro review (Munro, 2011) endorses the underpinning principles of the assessment framework, it nevertheless argues that it has succumbed to the pressures of proceduralized recording that has beset child protection processes in England. The review also notes that such a comprehensive assessment is not required in all situations:

> For some children, a brief assessment is all that is required prior to
> offering services and for others the assessment needs to be more in-depth,
> broader in scope, and take longer in order to get a sufficiently accurate
> understanding of the child's needs and circumstances to inform effective
> planning. (Munro, 2011: p. 41)

In response the review suggests a more flexible approach, based on professional judgement, that enables a proportionate assessment responsive to the needs of the child and their family.

The direction and guidance offered by the framework has been generally welcomed (Cleaver and Walker, 2004) although evidence also suggests that the framework cannot be a remedy for poor practice (Crisp et al., 2006). The introduction in 2007 of the Integrated

Children's System (ICS) built upon both the Looked After Children material and the framework for assessment material. The government argued that this development would allow for practice with all children to be harmonized and that the ICS would ensure that careful attention was paid to all the necessary dimensions of the child's life. In reality, however, the ICS system proved problematic and unwieldy, with practitioners frustrated at the amount of time needed and the limited scope for discretion presented by the system itself (White et al., 2009). Subsequently the government agreed to review the system with changes to the capacity of local authorities to develop the ICS in ways that reflected local needs and experiences.

The UK assessment framework is one way of gathering information to better understand the complex nature of an instance of child abuse or neglect and to work out the most appropriate service response. Internationally jurisdictions have utilized or adapted the UK framework, for example, Sweden has adopted it closely, whilst New Zealand uses the triangle as a visual prompt to engage practitioners with the ideas, but adopts a proportional response to the level of assessment based on the needs of the child and family. Other jurisdictions have developed their own ways of exploring areas of child and family needs, strengths and risks. For example, the Australian state of Victoria has created a useful package of resources that support professional practice relating to information gathering, analysis and planning (Victoria State Government, 2008). In a similar approach to the UK assessment framework, the Victorian assessment model identifies seven key domains from which key considerations are drawn and practice prompts provided. The following provides a brief example of each domain, but it is important to access the freely available original source for a full description of the key considerations and practice prompts[2]:

- The child or young person's safety
  ◊ Protection from harm
    o Does the child seem unreasonably or unexpectedly fearful?
- The child's stability
  ◊ Connection to primary caregiver
    o Who are the significant people in the young person's life?
- The child or young person's development and well-being

---

2 Available through the Victorian State Government website: http://www.cyf.vic.gov.au/__data/assets/pdf_file/0004/497965/best-interests-case-practice-summary-guide.pdf.

◊ Health and physical development
  o Does the child's emotional age match expectations of actual age and stage of development?
- The parent/caregiver's capability
  ◊ Parental attitude to the child
    o What are the basic rules for children in the family? Are these age and developmentally appropriate?
- Family composition and dynamics
  ◊ Who forms 'family' for this child?
    o Identify the key relationships within the family, including extended family, and significant prior relationships
- Social and economic environment
  ◊ Housing, employment patterns, income, informal community networks and cultural connectedness
    o Determine the desire or potential for change
- Community partnerships, resources and social networks
  ◊ Available community resources including sports
    o What service support does the family require to build social networks?

Creative ways of engaging with children have also been developed and implemented into statutory assessment practices. For example, the *Three Houses* (Weld and Greening, 2004) was primarily built to increase worker's engagement with children (figure 3.7). It offers a simple way of exploring worries, strengths and aspirations and takes workers away from the professionally-driven assessment formats. The introduction of the Three Houses has had an interesting impact on practice in New Zealand. Impressed by the way in which it engages discussion, practitioners have extended the use of the tool as a means of increasing knowledge of risks and strengths and working toward solutions – for example, as a way of exploring issues and solutions within family meetings, and even as an organizational management tool exploring agency strengths, worries and potential.

KEY PRACTICE QUESTIONS 3.2

1. What are the advantages and disadvantages of adopting established assessment models?
2. How does the use of assessment models strengthen or undermine professional judgement-making in child care and protection?
3. Would *The Three Houses* tool suit your practice style? If so, how might you use it?

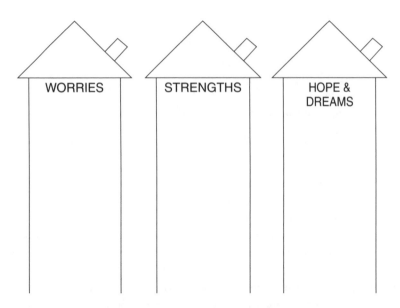

Figure 3.7 The Three Houses (CYF, 2011 adapted from Weld and Greening, 2004) reproduced with permission.

Decision-making processes in partnership with families

The third area we consider critical in the establishment of a strong practice system is the development of analytical decision-making processes that can be used in partnership with families. Every once in a while a new approach will emerge that fundamentally changes the way practitioners view their work and undertake their practice. It happened in 1974 when Reid and Epstein introduced *task-centred casework* to practice systems in need of clarity and a solid foundation of knowledge. It happened again when *family group conferencing* was introduced in 1989 as a way of involving extended families in decision-making for children at risk (see Chapter 4). Turnell and Edwards' *Signs of Safety*, introduced in 1999, is another example of an approach that has the potential to fundamentally change the way in which child welfare practitioners respond to families and work through the tricky business of child protection. For this reason we will dedicate the rest of this chapter to the signs of safety approach that builds partnerships with families and strengthens decision-making relating to children at risk.

Signs of Safety

Like most good practice approaches, Signs of Safety is build upon a set of important principles that guide the work (Turnell and Edwards, 1999: pp. 30–32). These are summarized as:

- *Respect service recipients as people worth doing business with.* Essentially you need to believe that families can change and conceive families as partners in safety.
- *Cooperate with the person, not the abuse.* Cooperation and building a relationship can occur without condoning the abuse.
- *Recognize that cooperation is possible even where coercion is required.* Statutory power potentially can be coercive. This power can, nevertheless, by utilized within a cooperative relationship with the family.
- *Recognize that all families have signs of safety.* No family is devoid of strengths, and most demonstrate signs of safety.
- *Maintain a focus on safety.* Practice should always increase safety.
- *Learn what the service recipient wants.* Understanding the family's concerns and dreams and incorporating them into planning will increase motivation for change.
- *Always search for detail.* Solutions can be found in the detail, rarely in generalizations.
- *Focus on creating small change.* Small, attainable steps create a context for success.
- *Don't confuse case details with judgements.* Understand and work with the facts. Reserve judgement until you are clear what is happening.
- *Offer choices.* Unnecessary coercion can alienate the family. Involve the family in developing ideas and choices.
- *Treat the interview as a forum for change.* The interactive relationship between the worker and the family, throughout all phases of engagement, can be a powerful vehicle for change.
- *Treat the practice principles as aspirations, not assumptions.* Principled practice is not formulaic. Principles guide us toward doing the right thing at the right time.

In developing the signs of safety assessment model, Turnell and Edwards recognized the deficiencies of risk assessments that focus only on danger and risk. Focusing on this exclusively is tantamount to 'mapping only the darkest valleys and gloomiest hollows of a particular territory' (1999: p. 49). Alternatively, their approach balances the gathering of information relating to harm and risk with areas of potential safety. All families have existing or previously demonstrated competencies and strengths. The signs of safety approach elicits information across the continuum between danger and safety allowing a more balanced and comprehensive assessment. It is important in this exploration to understand well the values, beliefs and meanings that family member ascribes to their experiences, and to search for exceptions to the maltreating behaviour. Harnessing strengths and resources within the family provides a context of hope where troubles can be worked through rather than the family (and the workers) being overwhelmed by the enormity of the problems faced. Having a focused goal orientation and working with the family's own goals has the potential to increase child safety, and scaling progress throughout the intervention helps to monitor how well the family is doing, providing a sense of progress for both family and worker. Having confidence in the family's willingness and capacity to carry out the plan is important before work begins. These practice elements have informed the assessment document which operates across a continuum between safety and danger.

Olmsted County in the US state of Minnesota has now been established as arguably the most enduring laboratory for Signs of Safety work, and has been innovative in the application of the assessment model (Lohrbach and Sawyer, 2004; Lohrbach, 2008). Building on the Turnell and Edwards original assessment template, they apply the tool in the context of family group planning conferences (Lohrbach and Sawyer, 2004) and also as a means of group supervision (Lohrbach, 2008). The template provides an excellent way of working through issues directly with the family, and indeed, this has been a primary aim of the tool from its inception. It is, nevertheless, Minnesota's application of the template as a means of strengthening practice decision-making in the context of a *group consultation* model that will be our focus in this chapter. The template (figure 3.8), in essence, forms the basis of a group supervision forum described by Lohrbach (2008: p. 20):

> They meet weekly for two to three hours; attendance is expected and
> required. The groups are facilitated by one or two supervisors. The meeting
> space includes chairs, a large whiteboard with the consultation template
> permanently inscribed, whiteboard markers, an eraser, and paper sheets also
> with the consultation framework template.

The process begins with the sketching of a genogram, a diagrammatic representation of the family tree – important for the worker who needs

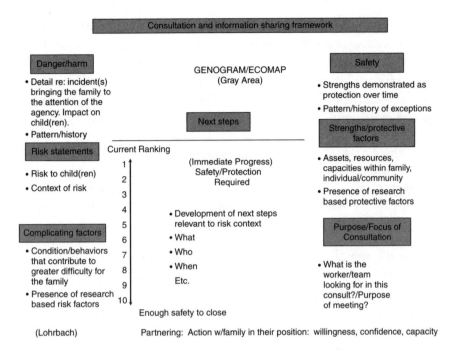

Figure 3.8 The Olmsted country group consult template (Lohrbach and Sawyer, 2004). Reproduced with kind permission of the American Humane Association.

to know who is who in the family. An eco-map or description of the services and resources surrounding the family is also helpful as it enables the team to see the worker's collaborative efforts in the case so far. The social worker briefly describes the family history and presenting issues, ensuring that the team is fully aware of the details of the situation and is able to effectively critique practice. The template is then completed, with an emphasis on clear, jargon-free recording that is both easily accessible to everyone in the team, and based on the actual facts of the situation. The section of *danger/harm* captures a succinct statement relating to the report of concern and any child protection past history. The *strengths/protective factors* capture the resources and capabilities within the family, while *complicating factors* might include disability within the family, or perhaps research-based risk factors such as maternal depression. The *safety* section is important in clearly articulating the ways in which strengths within the family are demonstrated as protection over time. This demonstration of protection is important. The family may have strengths, but it is essential to ascertain how these strengths translate into protection factors for the child. Exceptions are recorded here, for example, where the family has previously managed to overcome issues in non-abusive ways. There is a section for any *grey areas* where information may be lacking or incomplete at the time of the consultation. Lohrbach (2004: p. 22) describes the *risk statement* section as being comprised of two components:

> The first part of the statement articulates the worry (e.g. physical harm, sexual harm, death, illness, emotional harm) and the second articulates the context of the worry (e.g. a parent is using cocaine and their judgment and care may be impaired; without supervision or being watched over specific to the child's needs; when a parent hits or shakes the child).

Finally, the template provides *a scale* that helps the team understand present risk and safety, and a space for *next steps*. This is where the way forward is clearly outlined including tasks that may be necessary.

The group supervision consult provides the means by which practice responses can be respectfully interrogated in a disciplined and supportive way. The basis of interpretation is explored by team members who are interested and committed to a process of shared accountability. Embellishments or unwarranted speculation can be constructively questioned. Dissenting views are encouraged and good work is recognized and noted by the team. The nature of the group process also means that capability within the team strengthens as workers learn from both the positive and challenging aspects of each other's practice.

Increasingly, the signs of safety approach is practised positively in both statutory and non statutory child and family practice. Feedback from practitioners who use the tool is also positive (Field, 2008: pp. 16–17):

> It is easy to use; it makes sense; it's logical... it's a good process [social worker].
>
> The consult balances risks and strengths ...it breaks it down and the problems are separated from the strengths... it keeps us in the present and helps us decide on next steps. It has made a difference to our decision-making [social worker].
>
> The staff are comfortable with the process and they enjoy them... [the consult] is good for sharing information... it's enlightening and offers a new perspective [practice leader].
>
> It is the calm-down tool [practice leader].

┌─ KEY PRACTICE QUESTIONS 3.3 ───┐

1. Consider the principles which guide the signs of safety practice identified above. What challenges do they present when professionally responding to child maltreatment?
2. How might the exploration of both strengths and risk impact on a child protection enquiry?
3. What are the benefits and challenges in using a group consult model of supervision?

└──┘

Conclusion

In this chapter we set out to identify a set of practice initiatives that represent good practice within the area of child and family welfare. Whilst they inevitably represent only a fraction of the innovative practice approaches that have developed and will develop internationally, we would argue that they nevertheless capture three key areas necessary in the development of robust child protection practice systems: a clearly articulated knowledge framework that provides a high level vision of desired practice; engaging assessment models that address strengths, needs and risks; and analytical decision-making processes that can be used in partnership with families.

FURTHER READING

Knowledge frameworks

Connolly, M. (2007) 'Practice Frameworks: Conceptual Maps to Guide Interventions in Child Welfare', *British Journal of Social Work*, 37(5), pp. 825–37.

Trevithick, P. (2007) 'Revisiting the Knowledge Base of Social Work: A Framework for Practice', *British Journal of Social Work*, 38(6), pp. 1212–37.

Assessment models

Cleaver, H. and Walker, S. (2004) *Assessing Children's Needs and Circumstances: The Impact of the Assessment Framework*, London: Jessica Kingsley Publishers.

Department of Health (2000) *Framework for the Assessment of Children in Need and Their Families*, Department of Health, Department for Education and Employment, Home Office, London, accessible at http://www.dh.gov.uk/prod_consum_dh/groups/dh_digitalassets/@dh/@en/documents/digitalasset/dh_4014430.pdf.

Victorian State Government (May 2008) *Every Child Every Chance. Best Interests Case Practice Model. Summary Guide*, accessible at http://www.cyf.vic.gov.au/__data/assets/pdf_file/0004/497965/best-interests-case-practice-summary-guide.pdf.

Decision-making processes

Field, J. (2008) 'Rethinking Supervision and Shaping Future Practice', *Social Work Now*, 40, August, pp. 11–18, accessible online: http://www.cyf.govt.nz/about-us/publications/social-work-now.html.

Munro, E. (2008) *Effective Child Protection*, 2nd edition, London: Sage Publishers.

Turnell, A. and Edwards, S. (1999) *Signs of Safety: A Solution and Safety Oriented Approach to Child Protection Casework*, New York: W.W. Norton.

4

Family engagement strategies in child welfare

Key Points

- Internationally, systems of child protection have been working toward more collaborative ways of working with families. This has included harnessing the strengths of the wider kinship system in solution-focused practice.
- In some countries, this has resulted in a shift from professionally-based decision-making to family-led decision-making. Working with family strengths has been central to this approach.
- Whilst some countries have been able to support innovative practice, the involvement of families still remains a contested area of practice and presents challenges and opportunities for practitioners.

Whilst the development of family-minded practices in child welfare has influenced the ways in which statutory services respond to child abuse and neglect notifications and investigations, it has also influenced decision-making processes once a child safety issue has been established. In the past two decades, a distinct policy drive has occurred in the area of child protection and welfare practice – professionals are being asked to share decision-making power with families (Connolly, 1999; Morris and Featherstone, 2010). Across the globe (Burford et al, 2009), policy and practice has made moves towards participatory practices with the families of children at risk. This in part reflects greater recognition of the value of extended family involvement in good outcomes for children (Morris and Burford, 2007). It also responds to policy concerns to utilize the family resources and to explore family and friends care in preference to state care, thus strengthening family cohesion and support, whilst also reducing the burden placed on children's services. In some countries, Aotearoa New Zealand being the most noted in this regard, formal involvement of families in decision-making has been enshrined in legislation. In the UK, policy and practice expectations have promoted family involvement when children are in need of care and protection, and such practices have also received growing attention in Ireland, America and Canada (Burford, Connolly, Morris and Pennell, 2009). The Family Group Conference (FGC) model of practice has emerged as the most recognized innovation; a decision-making process that brings together the family, including the extended family, with the professional systems in a family-led decision-making forum. While originating in Aotearoa, the FGC has been adopted in other countries as a way of operationalizing notions of partnership and empowerment. In the US, such practice has been incorporated under the generic term of Family Group Decision Making (FGDM). These practices across the world reflect an important commitment toward family being involved in child welfare matters that concern them. They share a common vision of harnessing the strengths of the extended family and social network toward better outcomes for children at risk.

The Family Group Conference and its origins

In 1989 New Zealand introduced a radical piece of legislation that changed the way in which social workers responded to children at risk. It formalized a change in practice that recognized the centrality of family with regard to child care and protection decision-making, and fostered two important principles: the protection of the child, and the maintenance and strengthening of the family. The Family Group Conference model introduced by the legislation has now been widely adopted across child welfare systems internationally.

An FGC is a meeting to which members of the child's family, including the extended family, are invited. Typically, in New Zealand the FGC occurs once an assessment determines that the child is in need of care and/or protection. In other countries the positioning of the FGC is less certain – and dependant on local practices and needs (Nixon et al., 2005). Essentially, the FGC is a family-led model of decision-making which provides the family with the first opportunity to work through the care and protection issues. It has three main phases: the information sharing phase, the private deliberation phase, and the agreement phase.

During the information phase of the FGC, the care and protection coordinator, who convenes the FGC, is required to ensure that the family is provided with all the information needed to make

FAMILY GROUP CONFERENCE

Figure 4.1 Phases of the Family Group Conference

informed decisions about the care and protection of the child. The philosophy and aims of the FGC are explained, and information is provided about the concerns that have resulted in the FGC referral. This information is usually provided by the investigating social worker, although recent research suggests that a greater number of professionals are now participating in these meetings as information providers (Walton, McKenzie and Connolly, 2005). The information phase also provides the opportunity for the family to clarify any aspects of the investigation or have any questions that they may have answered.

The second phase of the FGC provides the opportunity for the family to deliberate in private. The deliberation phase is a significant departure from previous practices, providing the family with the first opportunity to sort through the issues and develop solution-focused plans and recommendations. In this phase, the professionals and any persons outside the family are asked to withdraw, and the family group is left alone to discuss the issues. The private family time is a critical component of the FGC. It firmly establishes the primacy of the family as the most appropriate group to make decisions about such family matters. It is the place where family members can talk honestly and openly to each other without professional oversight, and where family-led plans and decisions can be made. The processes needed to monitor the plan are also considered by the family, and contingency arrangements should the plan be unsuccessful.

Once this phase is complete, the full conference is again brought together to reach agreement on the way ahead. Various reviews of the evidence (Marsh and Crow, 1998; Burford et al., 2009 and Merkel-Holguin et al., 2003) suggest that, when provided with the opportunity, the significant majority of families can both create and agree a safe and appropriate plan.

The development of the FGC in New Zealand was strongly influenced by concerns relating to social disadvantage, and in particular the negative impact of child welfare practices on Māori, the Indigenous people of Aotearoa. An empowerment and rights-based paradigm rests at the foundation of family group conferencing in New Zealand. It is clear, however, that in the process of adopting the model, other countries have not always connected with the political and social heritage of the FGC (Morris and Burford, 2009). In its title the New Zealand *Children, Young Persons and Their Families Act 1989* reflects a commitment to family and their active involvement in matters of child welfare. Family is positioned at the centre of the child care and protection process, reinforcing the primary role family members have in the care of children, and placing responsibility on the state to support and strengthen the family. In the same year the 1989 Children Act in England and Wales was introduced. Whilst it set the scene for greater partnership work with families, the actual requirements for family involvement were more tentative, and whilst consultation with families was an expectation in the 1989 Children Act, how this was translated into practice was often a matter of local interpretation rather than reflecting legal duties and requirements (Ryburn and Atherton, 1996). Where the FGC has been adopted internationally it is mostly suggested as good practice as opposed to it being a legal requirement, or it is optional in law.

Whilst many saw the new legislation in New Zealand as ground-breaking, it was not without its critics. Debate began in earnest about whether the legislation adequately protected children, whether it truly empowered families, or whether it created an environment of covert disempowerment. Given family decision-making has been operating for over twenty years in New Zealand, it is useful to understand how practice has changed over time. Research into the FGC in New Zealand suggests a number of key findings (Connolly, 2006a; 2006b):

Micro practice issues:
- Within the FGC, creating a climate of honesty, and being upfront with families, increases the potential for the family to also deal honestly with the issues.
- Private family time provides the potential to promote within-family challenge and self-regulation.
- Power differentials in families inevitably exist and are likely to influence decision-making.
- Professional power dynamics also exist and can shift attention from the care and protection needs of the child.

Broader practice issues:

- Retaining children within their families of origin takes time, effort, and resources, and family-based solutions may rely on funding resources for their success. This raises the question of responsibility for retaining children within their family of origin, and the role of the state to protect this.
- Findings suggest that while the New Zealand legislation supports a family-led process, practice slippage toward professionally-determined processes is apparent. Practice positioning along an ideological continuum from family-driven process to professionally-determined process can be influenced by subtle changes as the practice matures.
- Frequent staff changes, although probably unavoidable in frontline practice, can have the effect of weakening organizational knowledge about the origins, aims and basic philosophy of the FGC movement. This contributes to ideological drift.

Results from this research suggests that over the passage of time, subtle changes in practice potentially undermines the strongly held family empowerment principles upon which the New Zealand legislation was based. For example, more professionals are found to be attending the FGC. There were times when professionals remained during the sacrosanct private family time. Concerned that families may 'flounder' without guidance, one coordinator noted:

I think I have a better handle on what it is that they need to know so that they are really confident about the task they have to do. So I will check on that process, and I pop in from time to time ... maybe even encourage them to have a professional with them if I feel that they would just flounder otherwise. (Connolly, 2006a: p. 533)

In addition, the New Zealand law states that children should be removed from their family only if there is a 'serious risk' of harm (CYP&F Act, s. 13[e]). The message here is that the state is expected to support the family plan unless it leaves the child at risk. Research suggests nevertheless a degree of professional pre-emption with respect to the decisions of the FGC, with the conference becoming a process that has to be gone through in order to get to court. Coordinators noted the importance of the social worker's philosophy with regard to the family-driven practice – 'still it hinges on the social worker having that same empowering belief – the notion of sharing and partnership with family' (Connolly, 2006a: p. 531). Whilst they felt that some social workers fundamentally believed in family empowerment, others struggled to accommodate a shift in the power base, and could still do 'the old kind of work with the old kind of values' (ibid).

Whilst it is likely that these changes contributed to practice efficiency and a better streamlining of the FGC process, it is also possible that it impacted on participants' perceptions of the locus of control. The concerns about professional management of family decision-making and the boundaries being set on the jurisdiction of family planning is an emerging international theme. Morris and Burford note in their discussions of developments in the US and the UK the evidence of professionals seeking to amend and adjust the implementation of FGCs and FGDM to ensure professionals can lead the decision-making processes (Morris and Burford, 2009). The positioning of the family in the decision-making process is critical to the impact of family involvement – and for many local processes this remains a difficult challenge, with family decision-making being at times predetermined by professional processes (Ashley and Nixon, 2007, Burford et al., 2009).

As practice develops over time, it is perhaps not surprising that professional processes have the power to influence practice along an ideological continuum. Even when workers identify strongly with family-led practice, they may find that drift occurs almost imperceptibly and is affected by a range of factors that may be within or outside their control. A set of practice models positioned across a continuum from family-driven to professionally-driven practice is, therefore, conceptualized (see Figure 4.2). The professionally-driven model best represents traditional practice where professionals dominate decision-making and the development of practice solutions, and there remains a heavy reliance on out-of-home care for children. On the other end of the continuum, family-driven practice represents family-led decision-making, practice transparency, family solution-focused processes throughout all phases of the work, and an emphasis on family care of children. Because practice responds to circumstance, it would be unlikely to be always fully operational at one or either end of the continuum. Essentially, family-driven practice may have professionally-driven elements. However, if it becomes consistently professionally-infused, as reflected in the model, it has the potential to lose important principles of family-driven practice and to be at risk of further shifting along the ideological continuum toward more fully professionally-driven practice.

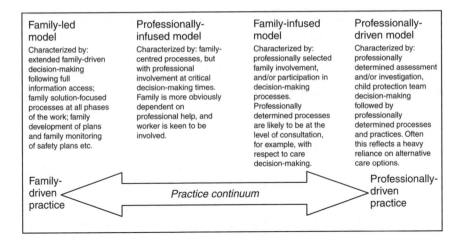

Family-led model	Professionally-infused model	Family-infused model	Professionally-driven model
Characterized by: extended family-driven decision-making following full information access; family solution-focused processes at all phases of the work; family development of plans and family monitoring of safety plans etc.	Characterized by: family-centred processes, but with professional involvement at critical decision-making times. Family is more obviously dependent on professional help, and worker is keen to be involved.	Characterized by: professionally selected family involvement, and/or participation in decision-making processes. Professionally determined processes are likely to be at the level of consultation, for example, with respect to care decision-making.	Characterized by: professionally determined assessment and/or investigation, child protection team decision-making followed by professionally determined processes and practices. Often this reflects a heavy reliance on alternative care options.

Family-driven practice ⟵ *Practice continuum* ⟶ Professionally-driven practice

Figure 4.2   Ideological continuum from family-driven practice to professionally-driven practice

---

KEY PRACTICE QUESTIONS 4.1

1. How do your local processes facilitate engagement with extended family where there are care and protection concerns?
2. What do you consider to be the strengths and weaknesses of family inclusion models such as the FGC?
3. Where on the ideological continuum would you place the child welfare agency you are most familiar with?

International developments in participatory practice with families

Whilst family group conferencing is nested within New Zealand legislation providing the primary means through which statutory decision-making occurs, it has also been adopted as a model of practice across international jurisdictions. In Australia, the state of Victoria first introduced family group conferencing in the early 1990s (Ban, 1994; 1996), and projects have developed across Australia since that time. In particular the FGC has been strongly promoted and developed in New South Wales, largely due to the commitment of UnitingCare Burnside who are well established in the provision of FGC programmes in partnership with the statutory services. Some Australian states, for example, Tasmania and Queensland, have also explicitly incorporated aspects of FGC practice within state legislation (Huntsman, 2006), and according to Anderson

(2005: p. 221) the 'FGC has grown from a practice innovation to an accepted, often heralded, service approach in child welfare'.

In the UK, developments in the use of FGCs has been mixed. Brown noted the marginal nature of many FGC services, sitting outside the mainstream provision of children's services (Brown, 2003). The recent inclusion of FGCs in various central government guidance documents has increased the profile of the model, and will lead to most local authorities hosting an FGC service.

The contested nature of family participation is nevertheless evident in the international developments of such practices and the accompanying evaluations, reviews and analysis. Aspects of policy and practice in the United Kingdom usefully illustrate the themes emerging from the growing body of literature about family inclusion. In England and Wales practice relies heavily on substituting family care with professional care when children are identified as at risk – a practice characteristic of the *rescue* model of child welfare (Marsh and Crow, 1998). The 1989 Children Act started a process of professionals exploring family involvement in the care and protection of children in their kinship network. The development of legal and policy requirements to support kinship care, set alongside expectations that family resolutions should be sought wherever possible (best illustrated by the 2009 Public Law Outline (MoJ, 2008)), has shifted the focus away from professional care towards a 'family first' response. As in New Zealand, however, such developments in the UK have also been the subject of challenge and debate. Critics argue that practice developments may be limited in their intention to truly share decision-making powers with families (Ashley and Nixon, 2007), and evidence indicates that families are offered little financial or practical support to care for children in their extended family network. This is often the case even when they are asked to become involved in planning and assisting professionals to meet the needs of related children (Family Rights Group, 2009). Most markedly in the UK public outcry at the tragic death of children living in their families (the Baby Peter case being a key example (Laming, 2009)) has generated debate about the feasibility of family care in some circumstances (Neary, 2009). Nevertheless, despite these localized, intra country debates family decision-making as a response to meeting children's needs has continued to generate interest and attention across the globe (Burford et al, 2009).

The US located American Humane Association had done much to spearhead practice interest and research into the use of the FGC as a model. In an early review of the evidence Merkel-Holguin, Nixon and Burford (2003: pp. 3–11) identified three broad themes within the research: implementation, process indicators, and outcome indicators, and their synopsis of the research indicated that the findings were positive (Table 4.1).

While Merkel-Holguin and her colleagues (2003: p. 11) noted a growing consensus on matters relating to issues of process and less on outcome, they concluded:

> Collectively, the results of the studies ... reinforce and realize many
> of the hopes held for FGC in child welfare. They undermine myths
> that have persisted to exclude families from planning processes. ... The
> evidence ... offers considerable support for the advancement of FGC and
> good reasons to further mainstream its practice. While there is only emerging
> proof that children are well-serviced in the long run, the early results
> compare favorably to those of existing practice.

More recently American Humane has commissioned an international review of the evidence, leading to the production of an annotated bibliography of studies from across the globe (Burford et al, 2009). The review adopted an inclusive approach to the evidence, reflecting the diverse range of material generated by the development of family inclusion practices. A systematic review would have resulted in few of the studies being considered – the embryonic nature of the policy and practice developments meant that studies were predominately local, small scale and developmental (Burford et al., 2009). Indeed where attempts have been made to adopt a systematic framework for a review of the evidence only a very limited number of studies met the criteria for evidence, resulting in a partial understanding of developments. The international review sought to adopt guiding questions in the gathering of evidence and the initial analysis of this evidence:

Firstly, what happens when families become involved in decision-making?
The evidence indicated that professionals need to recognize that whilst family decision-making may be a new *professional* practice it may be a well established family tradition. A number of studies sought to explore the relationship between established cultural traditions and

Table 4.1 FGC key research themes and findings (drawn from Merkel-Holguin et al., 2003)

Implementation	Process	Outcome
• Considerable effort and planning is needed during initial FGC implementation.	• Good preparation is essential to successful outcomes.	• FGCs compare favourably in terms of child safety measures.
• Strategic partnerships and alliances are essential.	• Families do respond positively when invited.	• The majority of children requiring safe placement go to extended family.
• Despite the developing interest in the FGC, the actual number of families accessing it remains low.	• Professional dominance of the FGC needs to be carefully monitored.	• FGC plans provide stability for the child.
• The FGC can also be used safely and successfully with the more demanding family problems (e.g. family violence).	• The majority (on average 95%) of the family plans are considered safe.	• Timely decisions and results are characteristic.
• The role of the coordinator is critical and has been found to be a predictor of a successful outcome.	• FGC plans provide a mix of formal service requests and family provided support.	• The FGC mobilizes the family support system and improves family functioning and communication.
• Wide variations in practice have been found internationally, and mostly it is introduced as 'best practice' rather than legally mandated.	• Rich, diverse and original plans are developed by families.	• One study indicates that the FGC may provide increased safeguards for other family members involved in the process.
• In general, service users (i.e. the families) have not been involved in service evaluations.	• An essential element of the FGC is the private family deliberation time.	
• The FGC as a model remains marginalized as a practice.	• The influencing power of the information-sharing phase raises key practice questions.	
	• Families appear to be satisfied with the FGC process.	
	• Families believe they have decision-making authority and 'a voice' in the process.	
	• Children's involvement in the FGC is variable.	
	• More men are becoming involved in the family process.	
	• Social workers and other professionals are satisfied with the process.	
	• Referral rates fluctuate and need further review.	
	• The FGC provides cost neutrality or savings.	

newly adopted professional approaches to family decision-making (see for example Koch, 2006; Desmeules, 2003; Cameron, 2006). These studies indicated that professional practices need to be responsive to traditions within families and communities – and to work with and harness established strengths within the family. Families responses reported in the studies indicated that families were positive about the opportunities to become involved in the processes that determine the future arrangements for the well-being of their child. Studies described family responses to the processes of FGDM and repeatedly identified both high satisfaction, and enhanced commitment and engagement with care and protection plans (see for example Morris, 2007; O'Sullivan et al., 2002 and Staples, 2007).

Secondly, what happens to children when family are included?

According to Welbourne (2002), whether or not child welfare agencies take seriously the rights of children is indicated by the degree to which the child has any input into decision-making processes that concern them. There is now a growing body of research and evaluation that is concerned with the experiences of children when family involvement strategies are adopted. A number of studies have explored the use of advocates for children and the practice skills needed to ensure children's participation is supported. Several make the point that attendance is not participation and that being listened to is not the same as being influential. However, the studies also indicated that children did feel that they had their say, and that family decision-making processes were preferred to professional processes (see for example Laws and Kirby, 2007; Holland and Rivett, 2008).

Alongside the consideration of children's participation in decision-making is the attention given to outcomes for children. Here the picture is complex; the developmental nature of many of the studies limited their ability to comment on long-term outcomes. Equally some research tools for testing outcomes (such as RCT) are open to criticism when used in this area of innovative practice. The studies reviewed suggested that children were more likely to stay within their kinship network, to experience increased stability and to positively rate the plans for their future (Sundell and Vinnerljung, 2004; Marsh and Crow, 1998; Morris, 2007). However, a small number of studies do question the impact of FGCs on longer-term outcomes, and raise important issues for those developing family-minded practices (Berzin, 2006; Sundell, 2003).

Thirdly, what happens to professional systems when family inclusion strategies are adopted?

The studies revealed complex issues about the capacity of professional systems to accommodate participative practices, or to capitalize on innovative service developments. The evidence suggested that there was some resistance rooted in a) the fit with other professionally-driven processes; b) perceptions and understandings of families where a child has care and protection needs; and, c) the drivers for professionals to embark upon innovative change when operating within a highly proceduralized and risk adverse environment (Morris and Burford, 2009; Brown, 2007; Holland et al., 2005).

More broadly, how FGDM and other family inclusion strategies are understood and captured in research and evaluation presents substantial challenges. The international review revealed real tensions in the appropriateness and relevance of existing indicators of impact when family participation is being examined. However, whilst research will continue to support and challenge the development of practice, it is nevertheless clear that a growing body of international research indicates the value of the involvement of families in decision-making.

KEY PRACTICE QUESTIONS 4.2

1. What might the issues be in adopting family group conferencing models across international jurisdictions?
2. What do you think some of the tensions in practice might be?
3. What skills would a worker need to develop to work inclusively with families where there are care and protection concerns?

Conclusion

Much has been said nationally and internationally about New Zealand's practice of family group decision-making epitomizing empowerment practice with families. Yet a closer examination of the work in New Zealand and increasingly in other countries suggests that practice may drift toward professionally-driven processes over time. It is clear that developments have the potential to flounder when there is professional reluctance to work in partnership with those using the services, and there are challenges in adopting the necessary strength-based approaches to harnessing the potential within the kinship network. Nonetheless, the evidence shows that where participative practices have been developed families are able to respond positively and to plan safely for their children. Returning to the original philosophy of the FGC, and rekindling its strength-based potential, can draw us back to family-driven practices. In the end, whilst families do rise to the challenge and responsibility of family decision-making, it is often the professional that provides the context within which this can occur.

FURTHER READING

Burford, G., Connolly, M., Morrison, K. and Pennell, J. (2009) *Annotated Bibliography on Engaging the Family Group in Child Welfare Decision Making*, American Humane Association, available from http://www.americanhumane.org/children/programs/family-group-decision-making/bibliographies/research-and-evaluation/.
Connolly, M. (1999) *Effective Participatory Practice: Family Group Conferencing in Child Protection*, New York: Aldine de Gruyter.
Pennell, J. and Anderson, G. (eds) (2005) *Widening the Circle: The Practice and Evaluation of Family Group Conferencing with Children, Youths, and their Families*, Washington DC: NASW Press.

USEFUL WEBSITES

The American Humane Association provides an excellent website for information on child welfare, and particularly Family Group Conferencing, available from: http://www.americanhumane.org/protecting-children/.
The New Zealand child welfare system (Child, Youth and Family) has a website resource for staff that provides information on all aspects of its practice, including family group conferencing. Available from www.practicecentre.cyf.govt.nz.

5

Statutory systems of care

Key Points

- State systems of care have changed dramatically over time and continue to evolve in response to a more developed understanding of the needs of children and young people at risk.
- There are three main types of state care: kinship care, foster care, and residential or institutional care.
- International trends suggest a move toward kinship care as a preferred care option.

Alternative care systems are constantly evolving. They are not static nor are they universal. They are constructs that respond to diverse cultural environments and the contexts within which they exist. Over the generations children have been looked after by people other than their parents – sometimes overseen by a government authority, sometimes not. Kin have always looked after the children of relatives. Although best practice in child care and protection reinforces the need to support parents in looking after their own children, there are times when this is not possible and the state intervenes to provide safe care. This chapter provides an overview of established options for children who enter state care systems, where relevant research is identified and some best practice messages are highlighted.

State systems of care have undergone a transformation over the past forty years. The emphasis on rescuing children from abusive and neglectful parents and placing them in residential care changed with the realization that children benefit from growing up in a family environment. As a result, foster family care became the preferred placement choice. More recently, the emphasis on family preservation and the recognition of the need for children to retain links to their own family networks, and a diminishing supply of foster caregivers, has led to an emphasis on kinship care (Gilligan, 2000a; Broad, 2001).

The majority of children require short-term care until they are able to return to their families. Yet longer-term care remains a reality when the goal of returning to parents is simply not possible. For some children a permanent arrangement through the use of adoption offers the stability and security they need, but adoption has historically been an outcome for only a small percentage of the care population.

Broadly, the care of children away from their parents can be grouped into three overarching types:

- Funded 'external' care by approved or registered caregivers who are unrelated or unknown to the child (foster care in family settings, residential care and therapeutic care are all examples of this category)
- Kinship care that utilizes care giving opportunities within the child's network (this includes care by family and friends and some private fostering arrangements)
- Permanent placement with alternative carers in a manner that formally creates new parenting arrangements for a child – usually through adoption.

But there is diversity across countries and states (Thoburn, 2007). In the UK the growing legal and policy attention focused on the use of kinship care has been less well supported by any commensurate growth of kinship care research and literature (Farmer and Moyers, 2005). Foster and kinship care are viewed in the US as temporary arrangements; the focus is on family preservation and reunification. Concurrent placement and wrap-around services are family preservation strategies designed to assist families to care for their children. Where reunification is not viable, guardianship and adoption are considered primary long-term outcomes.

In Australia, the process toward deinstitutionalization of children in care began in the 1970s, and within ten years foster care became the preferred option for children at risk (Bath, 2009). Like many other countries, Australia has increasingly supported kinship care in an attempt to ensure that children maintain links with their families of origin. New Zealand has followed a similar pattern of deinstitutionalization, particularly following the introduction of the CYP&F Act in 1989 when a strong push toward family care resulted in the closure of many of the larger residential care institutions.

There is evidence of recent increases in the numbers of children in care: in the UK for example England has experienced a 25 per cent rise in the numbers of children in the care system over the past decade. But this rising number appears to be due to an increase in the length of time each child is looked after, rather than a substantial increase in the number of children coming into care per se (DCSF, 2006). The number of Australian children in out-of-home care has risen significantly in recent years, from a rate of 3.1 per 1,000 children in 1998 to 6.2 per 1,000 in 2008, representing an increase of 115 per cent (AIHW, 2009). Somewhat contrary to this international trend, following reform efforts in New Zealand the number of children in care has reduced by 13 per cent in the period from 2006–2009 (Connolly and Smith, 2010).

This changing population, profile and the experiences of children in care and the implications for policies and practices will need to be underpinned by an allied development in research. This will assist professionals to better understand the care careers of children and the ways in which good outcomes can be supported.

Foster care

Countries and states use different terms to describe different care types for children in statutory care. Family foster care has been defined as:

> The provision of planned, time-limited, substitute family care for children who cannot be adequately maintained at home, and the simultaneous provision of social services to these children and their families to help resolve the problems that led to the need for placement. (Blumenthal, 1983: p. 296)

This provides a helpful definition that captures the broad nature of alternative foster care for children. Care in a family setting by unrelated carers can take a number of forms: emergency care, short-term care, planned respite care (increasingly recognized as a valuable resource for families where children have profound additional support needs) or long-term care. These different forms of foster care respond to different needs and consequently have different outcomes for children. There is a growing body of literature and research exploring the outcomes for children in foster care (Thoburn, 2007) and this section pays particular attention to the impacts and effects of short- and longer-term foster care. Sellick suggests that short-term care can usefully be described as *supplementary care;* short-term care aimed at assisting families to resolve difficulties and resume care, and long-term care can be seen as *substitute care;* longer-term care that replaces parenting by the birth family (Sellick, 2006: p. 69). As Sellick, Thoburn and Philpot rightly note (2004) measuring outcomes for children in foster care is complex and challenging and there are real difficulties in attributing particular outcomes to particular arrangements, given the complexity of the needs and experiences many children present. Nevertheless, the body of literature and research is now substantial and offers practitioners useful insights into effective provision and intervention (Wilson et al., 2004).

We have seen over the past decade changes in the profile of foster carers. The supply of potential foster carers has caused ongoing concern (Swain, 2005), and the challenging behaviour of children needing care can place enormous stress on existing carers (Hek at al., 2010). As a result, although the providers of foster care have historically been state funded agencies, recently there has been a growth of independent, not for profit and profit making foster care agencies. Sellick and Howell (2004) suggest there has been a steady growth of such providers in the UK and up to 18 per cent of children in care in the UK are now placed with independent foster care agencies. Similar developments are occurring elsewhere, with evidence of a mixed economy of care providers in a number of countries. In general, foster care services for children in Australia and New Zealand are provided either by the state or by non-government agencies that are funded primarily by the state. Both countries, however, have begun to see the development of profit making foster care agencies.

Short-term care

Early reviews of the research exploring short-term foster care (Berridge, 1997) suggested that short-term care was often used as temporary accommodation for children when they first come into care. Children tended to be younger and, in general, they were returned to their families within three months, although some stayed longer; the placement breakdown rate was low (one study suggests 10 per cent end prematurely); and children received good quality care. More recently Wilson et al., in their review of foster care research (2004), also suggested that short-term foster care had a relatively low breakdown rate, and generated a high degree of satisfaction. They suggested, however, that it might be more appropriate to reconsider how we view short-term foster care:

> Overall, on the evidence we have read, it seems clear that short term foster care is generally valued and not easy to prevent (for example, by improved family work). It may be best to see it as part of family support in the community rather than as an alternative to it. (Wilson et al., 2004: p. 23)

Sellick, Thoburn and Philpot, 2004 suggest that in these circumstances, where foster care is a form of family support, there is an important role for carers in maintaining children's connections with their birth family and in contributing towards the resolution of problems. These roles place additional demands on carers and in Chapter 6 we consider how effective systems of care can be supported, given changing demands.

Children's experiences of care differ and assumptions cannot be made about universal experiences of care away from home. For example, in the UK context evidence would suggest that children of mixed heritage are likely to experience higher placement breakdown rates than those experienced by white children. But professional responses to children may also be a factor with research suggesting that social workers are more likely to view short-term care for black and minority children as the first step in compulsory care whilst this is not necessarily so for white children (Thoburn, Chand and Procter, 2004). Sellick, Thoburn and Philpot (2004: p. 3), however, also note the absence of effective research into the experiences and outcomes for black and minority ethnic children, with research attention being focused on recruitment of ethnic minority foster carers rather than outcomes for children. Whilst it is clear that Indigenous children in both Australia and New Zealand are overrepresented in out-of-home care figures, there is a similar lack of research to inform better understandings of their experiences.

KEY PRACTICE QUESTIONS 5.1

1. Is short-term foster care best understood as a family support service?
2. What are the implications for practitioners, carers and families of short-term foster care as a family support service?
3. How can variations in the experiences of black and minority ethnic children be understood and addressed?

Long-term foster care

Long-term foster care is an option of out-of-home care that, ideally, provides the child or young person with a home for life (Schofield, 2002). But in reality, while some placements are enduring, in many longer-term care situations there are ongoing challenges in maintaining placement stability for children. A lack of stability places children at risk in terms of their development, attachment to primary caregivers, identity and sense of belonging, behaviour problems, and their ability to form relationships (Pecora et al., 2000; Wulczyn, Kogan and Harden, 2003). It has been argued that in the search for permanency, 'the importance of *belonging* as well as *security* in loving relationships (is) key' (Thoburn cited in Schofield, 2002: p. 260). In the UK and Australia, older children who have experienced maltreatment and who are unlikely to return home may be placed in planned long-term foster care until they reach independence. Concern at the insecurity of such placements is noted by Schofield (2001: p. 13), who concludes that despite the concerns, experienced and committed caregivers can provide children with 'stability and continuity of care' that can increase their ability to develop good relationships. Whilst some children needing ongoing state support may remain in long-term out-of-home care, in some jurisdictions, for example New Zealand, where carers are committed to providing a home for life, formalizing the care arrangement legally is encouraged. This provides the caregiver with the authority to care for the child independently of the state, but also allows negotiated packages of support based on what the caregiver and the child needs. As part of the ongoing support relationships the state will also make a commitment to 'being there' for the caregiver should future problems arise.

The body of literature and research about the outcomes of long-term foster care is complex, and it can be difficult to attribute particular outcomes to particular experiences. Biehal et al. (2009) explored the comparative outcomes of three types of permanent placements, including long-term foster care. Whilst they were able to identify higher rates of placement breakdown for long-term foster placements when compared to other forms of permanency, they also acknowledge that children in long-term foster care have different characteristics compared to children in other permanent arrangements such as adoption. They point out that:

> Children in long term foster placements generally enter these placements at a significantly older age than children enter adoptive placements. Previous research on both long term and adoptive care has found a strong relationship between age at placement and the risk of disruption.... (Biehal et al., 2009: p. 3)

Schofield in 2002, suggested that long-term foster care was, *'a much neglected area of social work practice and research'* (p. 259). But, as Sellick (2006) notes, foster care research has now moved from famine to feast, with a rich body of international evidence available to policy makers and practitioners. From this evidence emerges an important message; outcomes for children in long-term foster care are dependant on a complex set of variables and simple remedies cannot be found for addressing the risks of placement breakdown, poor outcomes and adverse consequences for future well-being. Rather, practitioners will need to explore the research as it relates to the children they support and develop responsive practices accordingly.

In response to the growth in the use of foster care, the UK government commissioned a programme of research into foster care, summarized in the overview by Sinclair (2005). The studies provided a rich insight into the experiences of children, carers and the outcomes of out-of-home placements. Simple conclusions cannot be drawn. The overriding message, nevertheless, is that foster care provides only one element of state responses to the needs of a child and it is important that the approach is responsive and sufficiently flexible to meet the challenges facing children entering public care.

Therapeutic foster care

Therapeutic foster care caters for children with special needs, particularly emotional and behavioural problems, children who have been sexually abused or who abuse others, or children with developmental and learning disabilities. Treatment or specialist care as a branch of foster care is a more recent development and in part is a response to the evidence that children entering the care systems are presenting increasingly complex and challenging needs (Hek et al., 2010; Salveron et al., 2010). A study of children in the English care system identified significantly higher levels of mental health needs, as compared to children who were not within the care system. Meltzer et al. (2003) found that 45 per cent of 5 – 17 year olds within the care system were assessed as having a mental health disorder. They found a prevalence of emotional disorders, conduct disorder and hyperactivity disorders. The researchers also found that these children were more likely to have physical health problems and educational problems.

Treatment focused foster care is, according to James and Meezan (2002: p. 1), 'a viable alternative to more restrictive settings for children and adolescents with serious emotional and behavioral disturbances'. Knowledge about the effectiveness of treatment foster care, however, is confounded by a number of factors, such as the variability of services, ecological factors associated with the child, the limitations of assessment tools, and narrowly defined outcomes that fail to account for a number of variables related to the child's functioning.

Multi-dimensional treatment foster care is a useful example of intensive, therapeutically minded foster care. It is a US model using a resilience framework as its theoretical basis. The approach responded to the challenge posed by children coming into foster care having witnessed or experienced situations of extreme trauma and adversity (drug use, domestic violence, extreme poverty, abuse and neglect). The model was subsequently adopted in the UK, and is being trialled with two groups of children – young children who need preventative interventions, and older children at risk of antisocial behaviour. Early indications are that this approach – intensive, integrated and rooted in a therapeutic understanding of needs – is having a positive impact. But there is also concern about the number of children failing to respond and benefit.

MacDonald and Turner's (2009) review of a sample of treatment foster carer schemes in the US also indicated that these intensive schemes can support positive outcomes for children; however they also acknowledge the limited evidence base and the high cost of these interventions.

Wrap-around services

Wrap-around services, also developed in the US, provide an alternative form of care for children with behavioural, emotional and mental health needs, particularly children and adolescents who are at risk of being placed in out-of-home care or group care. Wrap-around services are intended to stabilize the child through intensive interventions and active involvement of the systems of the child's life. Wrap-around services are 'individualized, community-based' services that enable them to be maintained 'in the least restrictive school and family settings' (Furman and Jackson, 2002: p. 1). With a child and family strengths-based focus, services are designed to 'wrap around' the child, and programmes are tailored to meet the specific, unique needs of the child as well as providing support, mentoring and advocacy for parents. The programmes encourage child and parent participation, respect the values and beliefs of the family, and are flexible and able to adjust to the changing needs of the child and family and, thus, provide access to appropriate services. Wrap-around programmes strengthen the integration of services and the collaboration between health, mental health, social services, probation, and special education services. While there are many advantages of such a system, as with concurrent placement, research has yet to determine outcomes for children.

Street et al. (2009) describe the outcomes of a UK service that sought to offer a joined-up integrated response, and to provide a team around the child. The service was multi disciplinary, and used a number of approaches – with an emphasis on attachment based responses. The children presented very high levels of need, with risky behaviour towards themselves, and towards others. This approach was rated positively by both carers and the children, and supported greater permanency and stability. It was acknowledged, nevertheless, that such approaches require a shared understanding across a number of disciplines, which is in itself a challenge. The small scale nature of the study means that it is difficult to draw broader conclusions for foster care practices and approaches.

Kinship care

Across many international jurisdictions, kinship care has become the favoured form of out-of-home care. Connolly (2003: pp. 3–4) outlines a number of cultural, practical and fiscal factors that have contributed to increasing interest in kinship care. These include a notable shift in orientation toward family-centred practices; the needs of the child and a greater awareness of the significance of the family's influence on the child's developmental needs, well-being, psychological attachment, and cultural and spiritual identity; increases in placement need as a consequence of fewer foster carers willing to undertake the task; and the exigency of foster care as an increasingly expensive and unmanageable option for the state. The influence of these factors varies from country to country (Hunt, 2008).

Whilst there may be concerns about the motivation for the increased development of kinship care, as a care type it is valued for its potential for maintaining contact between the child and family of origin and 'promoting cultural identity' (Doolan and Nixon, 2003: p. 17). Kinship care remains the most sympathetic care type with respect to the ideal of family preservation, and its potential contribution has already been considerable (Connolly, 2003). Kinship care has become the preferred option for children who cannot be cared for by their parents across international jurisdictions. The proportion of children in formal kinship care, nevertheless, still tends to lag behind foster care. In the UK figures suggest a relatively slow uptake of kinship care as an option – central government data indicates kinship placements have remained at around 11–12 per cent since 2005 (there are variations in this figure between the different countries within the UK). But very recent developments in UK legislation may see an upward trend in kinship care placements (Hek et al., 2010). By comparison, kinship care in Australia accounts for 24 per cent of care placements, 35 per cent in the US, and in New Zealand kinship care and foster care percentages are equally divided (Connolly, 2003). It is important, however, to note that these figures can only be considered as indicative. Definitional and sampling problems confound the potential to establish accurate figures and to make international comparisons.

Whilst research into kinship care has been somewhat limited, several aspects have been explored and comparisons made with traditional forms of foster care. In the UK two recent studies have explored the value of these placements for children (Farmer and Moyers, 2008; Hunt et al., 2008). Farmer and Moyers' research recognized the under-investment in kinship placements, but despite the lower level of state support offered to the placements, they were arriving at outcomes that could be compared with those of unrelated, better supported placements. Hunt et al. (2008) identified that for both children and their families kinship placements were a positive experience and were able to meet children's needs for safety. Importantly, children could also avoid a sense of 'being different'. A number of advantages of kinship care have been identified in terms of minimizing the disruption to the lives of children and maintaining family, social, and educational connections (Broad, 2001; O'Brien, 2000). A significant benefit of kinship care is that families are inevitably involved in decisions about what happens to children. This has the potential to enhance cultural responsiveness in placement decision-making, and maintain the child's identity and sense of belonging. Being with people that you know in a familiar environment also lessens the trauma of separation and retains links with parents and siblings.

Poverty is an issue that has a greater impact on kinship care than on foster care, Hunt and her colleagues (2008) and Farmer and Moyers (2008) both revealed the financial struggles facing kinship carers and the challenges created by financial hardship. With respect to children's well-being, however, the research is equivocal when comparing children in kinship care with children in low income relative and parent care households: '(C)hildren living with low-income relatives fare worse on some measures of well-being compared with children living with low-income parents, but on others they are doing just as well' (Billing, Ehrle and Kortenkamp, 2002: p. 1).

As a recent survey of kinship care policies in England and Wales identified, families are being asked to assume responsibilities for children without the necessary accompanying practical, financial and emotional support (FRG, 2009). This echoes the message emerging more generally from the body of kinship care research that families are being asked to care without support and this implies a transfer of the financial burden from the state to families, many of whom are already low income households.

The safety of children in kinship care is an issue that continues to be debated. Writers have suggested that it may be more difficult for relatives to enforce protective restrictions with respect to parental contact than it is for foster caregivers (Rubin, Downes, O'Reilly, Mekonnen, Luan, and Localio, 2008). Aldgate and McIntosh (2006) also caution against a 'cozy view' of kinship care that may assume that families are 'risk-free zones'. Concerns relating to safety in particular, focus on intergenerational child abuse and neglect and poor parenting practices (Hunt, 2008). Claims that relatives are as poorly functioning as the children's biological parents, however, are not necessarily substantiated (Terling-Watt, 2001). Perhaps some fears can be mitigated by the fact that in a number of cases where children are reported to be at risk, it is relatives who contact child welfare agencies, giving 'testament to families' desire and capacity to protect' (Berrick et al., 2000). Yet the number of high profile cases of children experiencing injuries, some fatal, at the hands of extended family members continue to test these assertions. It is important to remember, nevertheless, that such cases are rare, and it is useful to consider them in the context of Worrall's (2001) study where family members were instrumental in taking steps to protect children at risk. It is also important to recognize the additional difficulties that kinship care can bring to family dynamics. Notifying care and protection services or the police of concerns regarding the well-being of children can create rifts in the family network, whilst taking responsibility for the care of the child can result in family conflicts and compromises for caregivers.

A number of studies have examined the different outcomes between kinship and non kinship care in terms of the well-being of children. Summarizing the results of these studies, Hunt (2008: p. 14) notes:

> Findings are broadly positive and while it cannot be said for certain that children in kinship care do better than those in non-related care it seems at least that, on balance, they do no worse. And while there may be little enough positive evidence ... the absence of recent negative evidence is also not without significance.

Although there may be contradictory experiences for families in the context of kinship care, a recent systematic review of the research supports the practice as a 'viable out-of-home placement option' (Winokur et al., 2009: p. 6).

Residential care

Despite the general trend toward deinstitutionalization, residential care continues to be an option for some children in some circumstances. Several studies provide evidence to suggest that residential care has positive outcomes. Factors associated with success include well-planned care, longer time spent in the programme, face-to-face contact with the family worker, and contact with family. Pre-intake variables are also implicated, including age and living situation (Maluccio et al., 2000). Whilst acknowledging that those who lived in group care or orphanages in the past differ from today's population, studies of adults reveal good outcomes: 'happy memories' and higher levels of success in terms of 'education, income and attitude towards life' (Maluccio et al., 2000: p. 45), as well as a stated preference for orphanage rather than foster care (McKenzie, 2003). There are, nevertheless, ongoing concerns about the well-being and welfare of children cared for in residential institutions (Kendrick, 2008). Dixon (2007) suggests that young people leaving residential care experience a range of poor outcomes in relation to health, education, employment and well-being. Recent disclosures relating to historical abuse in residential units (see for example the recent UK concerns about abuse and the Jersey and Scottish investigations into state run care homes) have also raised anxieties about the safe and appropriate care of children who live in group homes.

Not all children will benefit from residential care, although for some children with specialized needs, residential care can have positive outcomes (Fulcher, 2001). For example, better outcomes can be achieved by focusing on the resilience of children supported by the institution's capacity to offer a secure base, their potential with respect to the development of both educational and social competencies, and the reinforcement of positive values (Daniel et al. cited in Fulcher, 2001). Short-term residential care has received limited research attention. Nevertheless, residential services frequently provide emergency care, assessment services, and accommodation preparatory to fostering or independence, or for young people on remand (a maximum of three months for youth justice clients in New Zealand) (Geraghty, Laing and Warren, 2002). Little is known about the quality of care or the long-term outcomes of this form of intervention, and it is critical for research to explore the issues related to this type of care and the experience of people who are exposed to it. Likewise, some groups of children (children with particular support needs, disabled children and asylum seeking children) may all need and be placed within residential units. Research about the outcomes for children cannot assume a commonality of experience, and early indications are that some children such as asylum seeking children will have specific needs and high risks of poor outcomes (Kohli, 2007).

In recent years, influenced by international 'best practice' ideologies, which focus on diminishing levels of intervention, Australia and New Zealand have moved away from the provision of residential care services in favour of more family-oriented care options. This has been highly appropriate given the needs of the majority of children requiring state intervention. Nevertheless, it leaves a service gap for children and young people with special needs that cannot be accommodated within family-type systems of care. As a consequence, new residential facilities have been developed with the aim of providing more specialized and effective services for young people, with an emphasis on therapeutic services that reflects the different needs of different groups (Brucker, Easterbrook-Smith and Martin, 2003). In the UK arguments have been made for rethinking residential care and in the wake of a series of revelations of abuse within care homes, there is a concern that the potential benefits for some children of residential care may be lost

(Smith, 2009). The emergence of approaches that utilize the concepts and ideas of social pedagogy have a direct relevance for the future development of residential care and residential staff. This approach has roots in European models of practice and suggests new ways of bringing together the social, educational and emotional responses to children's needs (Petrie et al., 2006). As Smith notes in his analysis of new directions for residential care:

> Social pedagogic approaches incorporate all the elements required of a coherent philosophy of care, a broadly social educational paradigm based around the concept of upbringing, an emphasis on life space and activity based work, the assertion of the centrality of personal relationships and the need for well-qualified, reflective and reflexive practioners. (Smith: p. 175)

Adoption

When children cannot live with their parents or within their extended family, another option of long-term care is adoption. When a child is adopted, the biological parent's legal rights are irretrievably terminated and the adoptive parent becomes the legal parent in all respects. Attitudes toward adoption have changed over the past decades. More liberal attitudes to sole parenthood have created a climate where more women have chosen to look after their children as opposed to seeking adoption as an alternative. In some jurisdictions a greater degree of openness between the parties is encouraged, although this is invariably undertaken on an informal basis and the degree of openness is dependent upon agreement between the birth parents and the adoptive parents.

Countries vary in the ways they promote adoption for children. The US and the UK are active in their promotion of adoption, supporting both legislative and funding incentives (Connolly and Cashmore, 2009). In 2008 there were almost five thousand children adopted in the UK, an increase of 4.4 per cent on the previous year, and 7 per cent more than there had been in 1998 (Office for National Statistics, 2010). In Australia and New Zealand adoption is less common. In Australia there has been a significant drop in the number of adoptions from almost 10,000 in the 1970s to less than 500 in 2008/09 (AIHW, 2010). Significantly, in the 2008/09 year over 60 per cent of the adoptions were inter-country adoptions. Whilst the number of adoptions in Australia overall have reduced over time, they have nevertheless remained relatively stable since the mid 1990s with between 400–600 adoptions occurring per year. New Zealand has also seen a reduction in the number of adoptions over time. In 1968, 2,617 New Zealand children were adopted by people unknown to them. Over the next twenty years, however, the number declined, falling to a low of 62 non-kin adoptions in 2009, although the average for the past decade has been 88 per year. Accurate inter-country adoption statistics are difficult to ascertain in New Zealand as they are sometimes finalized overseas but there are, nevertheless, indications that numbers are decreasing. In 2007 there were 56 inter-country adoptions dropping to 16 in 2009.

Conclusion

Over time, there have been shifts in the way the state has responded to out-of-home care. An early reliance on residential care gave way to a preference for family foster care which, until relatively recently, has been the traditional system of care for children at risk. The growth of kinship care in some jurisdictions has created a situation in which research and policy is struggling to keep pace with developing practice. It is increasingly clear that child welfare systems face considerable challenges. This is not only with respect to meeting the needs of children and the people who provide care but also in terms of better understanding the systems of care and how they impact on the people involved.

FURTHER READING

Owusu-Bempah, K. (2010) *The Wellbeing of Children in Care: A New Approach for Improving Developmental Outcomes*, Abingdon: Routledge.

Sinclair, I., Baker, C., Wilson, K. and Gibbs, I. (2005) *Foster Children: Where They Go and How They Get On*, London: Jessica Kingsley Publishers.

Social Work Now (children in care special edition) available online at http://www. cyf.govt.nz/documents/about-us/publications/social-work-now/social-work-now-41-dec08.pdf.

USEFUL WEBSITES

The Australian Institute of Health and Welfare reports a range of statistics which focus on children, youth and families, including information relating to out-of-home care. It is retrievable at http://www.aihw.gov.au/childyouth/index.cfm.

The UK Department for Children, Schools and Families *Every Child Matters* website provides a range of information relating to out-of-home care for children. It is retrievable at http://webarchive.nationalarchives.gov.uk/20091115062648/dcsf.gov.uk/everychildmatters/safeguardingandsocialcare/childrenincare/fostercare/fostercare/.

6

Supporting family-based systems of care

Key Points

- Caring for children who cannot remain with their parents, either as formal, paid caregivers or as kinship carers, places considerable strain on carers and families and requires skilled social work support
- Whilst there are factors that seem to support the likely success of a placement, outcomes are related to the individual needs of the child and require careful consideration of issues such as contact with birth families, ongoing support for caregivers and accurate assessments of children's needs
- Kinship caregivers provide an important service to the state in terms of caring for children at risk. In general, however, kinship care is not as well supported as other systems of statutory care and kinship carers face the challenges of poverty, poor support and complex family dynamics.

Social workers and other professionals play their part in responding to the needs of children in care, but it is the statutory caregivers who provide the most essential day-to-day care and attention. Studies describe the characteristics and motivation of foster caregivers, the recruitment and assessment methods, as well as the training programmes and support services they receive. Although kinship care is a relatively new form of state care for children, research has provided insight into the conflicts and dilemmas that kin caregivers in particular face. Whilst the use of residential or group care has declined, the specialized needs of children in this form of care require well-trained caregivers with an extensive knowledge base and level of expertise.

The difference between what is asked of 'ordinary' families and what is asked of foster families is perhaps epitomized by Berridge (1997: p. 7), who contends that, 'foster carers look after some of the most difficult, demanding, rejected and abused children and young people in our society. They offer homes to other people's children with little public recognition and there can be few more challenging endeavours'. In the past, foster caregivers were expected to fulfil the role of a substitute parent, particularly where long-term foster care could be seen as 'quasi-adoptive'. More recently, in recognition that foster care placements are frequently short-term rather than long-term, the role of the foster caregiver has expanded to include the need to work alongside a child's birth family. Yet the foster caregiver's role involves a number of difficulties and ambiguities. For example, Triseliotis et al. (2000: p. 2) argue that they are, 'expected not only to provide family care without becoming too attached to the children, but also to deploy high skills and expected to care for some very troubled and troublesome children and young people'.

Increasing use of kinship care, particularly in Indigenous and ethnic minority communities, raises a number of issues that are not part of the foster family dynamics. Fostering within the extended family has its roots in traditional practices of kinship care; child care options have always included informal placement with grandparents or other family members. Attempting to model this system along the lines of formal foster care creates tensions within family networks. The legal issues and processes alone increase the stress for families trying to find a solution to the needs of children who are neglected, maltreated, or have behavioural problems. Furthermore, the family member who elects to take responsibility for the child may be faced with a number of emotional issues: shame and guilt due to the parent's state of health or behaviour, social stigma, and a sense of intrusion and loss of privacy as statutory agencies become involved (McFadden, 1998).

The characteristics of caregivers

The profile of the different groups of caregivers – foster carers, kin carers and residential carers – do differ, and assumptions cannot be made about shared needs and experiences. As the placement of children within kinship networks gains focus as a preferred or possible option, increased attention is being given to the characteristics and experiences of family and friends carers. Overall knowledge about what makes a 'good carer' still requires further development (Hek et al., 2010) and despite the significant use of statutory care for children, writers have also noted the 'shortfall in the research and evidence base for practice' (Cashmore and Ainsworth, 2003: p. 5).

Foster caregivers

Sinclair, drawing on a study of foster carers in the UK (2005) suggests that the profile of foster carers has changed little over the decades, with 'traditional' family forms being the common enduring feature. This study questions how well the fostering task can be accommodated by contemporary family life that may not consist of two parents and external paid employment. For the most part, the characteristics of foster caregivers reflect the gender division in households where women are the primary caregivers and men take a secondary role. Only a small minority of single men are found among the caregiving population (Triseliotis et al., 2000). A study of independent foster carers (a growing aspect of foster care provision) found that the vast majority were heterosexual, married couples with only a small minority of unmarried partners and even fewer same sex couples (Sellick and Howell, 2004). In the US, most foster families are two-parent families, occupations ranging from professional through to unskilled (Orme and Buehler, 2001).

Historically the proportion of foster caregivers from minority ethnic groups in the UK has caused concern and has led to a number of targeted schemes that aim to specifically recruit and support black and minority ethnic foster carers. Such schemes do appear to be successful and as a result the profiles of carers in local authorities in the UK vary according to the recruitment campaigns that have been developed. Earlier studies from the US note that 88 per cent of foster caregivers were white, whereas later studies reveal 28 to 58 per cent are African American (Orme and Buehler, 2001).

Foster carers do face a challenging and demanding task and as Wilson et al. argue (2004) the overall stability of the profile of carers may well reflect the challenges of combining external paid work with the demands of caring for a foster child, and that one way forward may well be to more explicitly acknowledge foster caring as work and reward it appropriately.

Kin caregivers

The characteristics of kin caregivers differ from those of foster caregivers. In general, kin caregivers tend to be older women, often maternal grandmothers or aunts, who already have a close relationship with the child; uncles, and siblings also take on the role. Farmer and Moyers (2005) found that in their study of kinship carers in England, almost half (45 per cent) of carers were grandparents, with aunts and uncles constituting the second largest group. Research relating to the characteristics of kinship caregivers is underdeveloped in Australia, although the particular pressures for Indigenous carers who experience higher rates of disadvantage and poverty have been noted (DOC, 2007). Recording limitations make it difficult to accurately ascertain the nature of statutory kinship caregiver relationships within New Zealand, however, when relationship is recorded grandparents are the primary caregiver (44 per cent) followed by aunts (22 per cent).

Perhaps inevitably, kin caregivers are more likely to be committed to the child than non-kin caregivers. Care distinctions have been drawn by some kin caregivers: 'I'm raising him, I'm not caring for him... he's part of my family' (Benevolent Society, 2009). Hence, taking the child into care is viewed as, 'a natural loving response, in part to prevent "their" child from being taken away from the family' (Broad, 2001: p. 40). A UK study (Doolan, Nixon and Lawrence, 2004) found that half the children being cared for by grandparents had contact with their parents (39 per cent had daily contact). A recent New Zealand study of grandparents raising grandchildren found that 20 per cent of the children had no contact with their parents, 25 per cent reported contact as irregular, and 17 per cent as regular (Worrall, 2009).

Family and friends carers experience higher levels of disadvantage with more lone carers, overcrowded housing and poor health being evident (Farmer and Moyers, 2005; Worrall, 2009). This reality of poor and disadvantaged families taking on the care of children who may have had difficult life experiences and need considerable support raises real implications for how the local and national policies support family and friends carers and how social workers respond to their needs.

Family dynamics can create additional problems for kin caregivers and add stress to their role (Farmer, 2009a). Relationships between caregivers and the parents of the child can be problematic, especially when caregivers are critical of parents' standards of care, have difficulties in establishing boundaries, regulating, supervising and maintaining contact with parents, or when the child is reluctant to spend time with the parent. Worrall (2009: p. 5) also notes feelings of grief experienced by kin caregivers:

> Grief arises out of disappointment that their children and/or grandchildren have gone to prison, death of their own children; death of spouses; broken

marriages; lives lost to drugs and alcohol and grief in respect of injuries the children will not recover from, for example, brain injured shaken babies. There is also sorrow and anger that they have to face challenges to their custody in court from their own children and the cost of this – money taken that could be spent on their needy grandchildren.

Assumptions cannot be made about the commonality of experience across countries for kinship carers. Farmer's work comparing her UK study with findings from the US suggests that there are both differences and similarities, and this reinforces Hunt's recommendation that local authorities and central government policy makers must consider carefully the experiences of kinship carers and construct policies and practices accordingly (Hunt et al., 2008). Comparisons between kinship and traditional foster care raise questions about minimum standards of care and accommodation. Yet when statutory agencies are involved, kin caregivers experience loss of privacy, autonomy, and even control over what happens to the child, (Family Rights Group, 2009). Many issues remain concerning kinship care, particularly the question about the suitability of poor families to care for children when family circumstances, including poverty, may, in fact, have contributed to the neglect of the child (O'Brien, 2000), an issue we will consider later in the chapter. Nevertheless, research suggests that children are likely to do no worse in kinship care than in foster care situations (Hunt, 2008), and they have the considerable advantage of genealogical continuity.

Motivation

In general, foster caregivers view fostering as an opportunity to care for underprivileged children (Rhodes, Orme, Cox and Buehler, 2003); for some, the sense of altruism can be associated with their religious beliefs, whilst others may have childhood experiences that help them to identify with this group of children. They are also interested in extending their families and their child caring role, and will have an ability to foster. Studies suggest fostering is an option for couples who have been unable to adopt (Berridge, 1997; Triseliotis et al., 2000).

Colton and Williams's study of global trends in family foster care (2006) suggest that two challenges exist in the recruitment and retention of foster carers: motivation and capacity. There are different responses to foster care in different countries, and these reveal the challenges of developing effective foster care provision. Families may have the desire to care but not the emotional or practical capacity to do so, or cultural and traditional values may not support caring for unrelated children within the family. They point to a global shortage of foster carers and the complex challenges facing services in recruiting and retaining carers. Maluccio and Ainsworth (2006) suggest that greater clarity is need for foster carers about their role and the expectations placed upon them and the increasingly complex needs children entering the care system present (Quinton, 1998) further reinforces this need for reflection and review.

Motivations for fostering are more complex for kin caregivers. Often asked to take a child in an emergency situation, they may do so out of a sense of family obligation or duty and an interest in family preservation (Doolan et al., 2004). Perhaps this reflects Allan's (cited in Schofield, 2002: p. 7) view of the 'diffuse and enduring solidarity' of kinship ties and the persistence of kinship 'obligations, rights, privileges and responsibilities'. In the UK family members were believed to have, 'initiated the kinship care placement, to prevent "their" child being "taken from the family" and placed in care' (Broad, 2001: p. 38). Hunt's study of kinship carers suggests that for many the decision to assume the care of a child was instinctive rather than a measured, reflective decision. Carers were often motivated by having a close relationship with the child prior to the child needing care, and the study suggests that few regretted their decision – even when the placement subsequently broke down (Hunt, Waterhouse and Lutman, 2008).

Creating a positive out-of-home care environment for children

Specialist skills are required to work within statutory systems of care. Creating a positive care environment for the child involves the assessment and support of suitable caregivers, the process of making sure that the fit between the child and caregiver is the best that it can be, the management of complex dynamics relating to the rights of children, parents and families, and the ongoing support needed to sustain the placement. The removal of a child from a parent is a serious action and once taken it is incumbent on the state to make sure that the care environment meets the child's care and safety needs. Yet research consistently identifies a number of factors that compromise good child welfare practice. These include the high demand for services, heavy caseloads, low levels of staff training and support, and lack of resources.

A review of the literature undertaken by Wilson et al. (2004) suggests that children in public care systems face difficulties in relation to health, safety, emotional well-being, education, forming close relationships and developing a positive identity. These are all matters that are connected to the practice of the social workers, and the care offered by foster carers and other care staff involved with the family. As numerous studies reveal, both children in care and their foster caregivers have historically been poorly served by social workers and by care systems more generally. Concerns about poor outcomes for children have led to high profile initiatives, such as the Care Matters programme driven by the UK Government (2007; 2008; 2010). Such initiatives are seeking to promote stability for children in care, focus attention and support for better educational, health and emotional outcomes and increase levels of inspection to ensure that services meet requirements.

Caregiver skills and experience

Foster caregivers require special if not extraordinary skills to protect and nurture children, meet their developmental needs, support their relationships with their families and collaborate with professionals. Whilst standards for kinship foster care have now been developed in many countries (Chipman, Wells and Johnson, 2002), in the UK, there is a need to develop kinship care-specific policies, guidelines, preparation and training programmes to assist kin caregivers to achieve successful outcomes for the children who come into their care (Family Rights Group, 2009, Doolan and Nixon, 2003; Brudenell and Savage, 2000; Spence, 2004).

Foster caregivers have an important role in assisting children to acquire a sense of secure attachment and well-being and to foster a sense of resilience within the child. This includes encouraging and managing contact with families, encouraging educational experiences and attainment, peer relationships, hobbies and talents, and ensuring that children have opportunities to develop skills in problem solving and social competence (Gilligan, 2000a). As Schofield (2002) argues, these goals will be best achieved by recruiting caregivers who can provide a secure environment in which children can feel that they belong to a family, are able to resolve the loss and trauma of the past, to develop the ability to love, and the coping skills and adaptability that will enhance resilience. Drawing on a number of case studies, Schofield (2001: p. 16) contends that foster caregivers, 'provide a buffer against the worst consequences of early damage.... The emotional availability of carers and their capacity to stay with these children through thick and thin demonstrated the role of relationships in promoting resilience'.

A number of predictors of successful outcomes for foster care have been identified, including: older caregivers with experience in fostering; caregivers who do not have children of the same age and sex as the foster child; the maintenance of contact with parents and social workers; the receipt of preparation and training; access to a range of resources; and being well supported, both formally and informally (see for example, Rhodes et al., 2003) and able to offer authoritative parenting combined with real engagement with the child's life. This is a complex area nevertheless and it is difficult to establish 'hard facts' about the indicators for a successful placement. So much depends on the particular needs of the child and the capacities and approaches adopted by the carers and the professionals. Working with adolescents and children with special needs requires additional skills. As children get older the rates of placement breakdown gets higher but then reduces for older teenagers – in part because placement breakdowns may be dealt with by planned moves into independent living arrangements (Sinclair, 2005).

Sinclair suggests in his review of the evidence that:

> ...overall the message is that both child and carer contribute to the
> outcome. Each may bring out the best or worst in the other. In the end,
> the outcome of the placement depends on the relationship that develops.
> (Sinclair, 2005: p. 82)

Assessing caregivers

An important step in providing safe and nurturing out-of-home care for children involves the assessment of caregivers. In general, the assessment of caregivers has followed a traditional pattern regardless of the caregiver's relationship with the child. Hence potential kinship caregivers would be assessed in the same way as potential foster caregivers who have no pre-existing relationship with the child or family. Such caregiving assessment models usually explore the caregiver's home environment; motivation; history (including criminal history); abilities and strengths; and any barriers that might undermine their ability to care (for example, age, health, attitudes). Writers, however, have questioned the generic assessment of caregivers suggesting that fundamental differences between kinship care and stranger foster care require different assessment processes and approaches (Doolan et al., 2004). Indeed a recent exploration of kinship care in Australia (SPRC, 2009) has argued for the development of distinctly different processes for kin and non-kin:

> Kinship care practice models used by out-of-home care agencies need to be different from foster care practice models. In foster care, the carer has made an informed decision to take on the child after an intensive training and assessment process. In kinship care, placements are frequently unexpected, the carer often has a pre-existing relationship with the child and birth parent, and the assessment and authorization of the carer may happen while the child is already living with them. (Benevolent Society, 2009: p. 1)

It is clear that across international jurisdictions systems of child welfare have been exploring ways of developing their assessment processes to accommodate the needs of kinship caregivers. In the UK, according to Farmer and Moyers (2008), a lack of clear policy direction with respect to the management of kinship care has resulted in a range of responses from local authorities to the particular needs of kinship caregivers. Some have made efforts to develop clarity around their needs, whilst others remain vulnerable to variations in practice. Some countries have progressed efforts to develop specific processes for kinship caregiver assessments. For example in New Zealand distinctly different caregiver assessments are undertaken depending on the nature of care and the relationship of the carer to the child. Whilst foster caregivers continue to be assessed through traditional methods, different areas are explored with kinship caregivers (CYF, 2010a) and a significant step in the process includes a whanau hui (a family meeting similar to a family group conference) where extended family are brought together to contribute to the assessment process (CYF, 2010b). This resonates with other culturally responsive approaches 'that changes the emphasis from "approving" to "enabling" carers to provide care for the child' (SPRC, 2009: p. 39).

Placement decisions

Parents provide for a child's physical, emotional, psychological, social, cultural and spiritual needs, and a well integrated family environment provides the basis of a child's safety and sense of identity, self value and belonging. When the state intervenes and removes a child from parental care the change may be judged by how well it provides a child with those elements of this well integrated, family-oriented response. Placement decisions are critical with respect to providing this kind of response.

Whilst kinship placements mostly result from family offering to care for a relative's children, when a child cannot be placed within the family system foster placement decisions involve assessing and matching the needs and potential of the child with the qualities and characteristics of the foster caregiver; establishing the goals of the placement, including contact with the birth family; monitoring outcomes and reviewing decisions; and providing training and support for foster caregivers (Triseliotis et al., 2000; Sinclair, 2005). Ideally, placement decisions involve the child and their parents/caregivers and incorporate information about the family and the child from the perspectives of social workers, education and health professionals. As Sinclair points out, however, no assumptions can be made about the existence of shared agreements about how best to meet a child's needs. Nor do all those involved have the same levels of experience and knowledge. Aspects such as location (e.g. links to family and neighbourhood) and ethnic, cultural and religious practices also need to be considered (Sinclair, 2005; Wilson, 2004). The age of the child is important with problems connected to attachment, separation and loss increasing as the age of the child at placement increases (Sellick et al., 2004). Yet crisis or emergency situations create difficulties in terms of managing the 'fit' between the child and the foster care-givers. A study of teenage placements suggests that placements made quickly, in response to emergencies were more likely to experience disruption and usually this was as a result of the young person's behaviour (Farmer et al., 2004). Clearly, responding quickly to the needs of children whilst balancing the need for careful and detailed attention to the care arrangements is a practice challenge for social workers, and for foster carers.

Whilst emergency placements are usually short-term, more time and consideration can be given to permanent placements. These placements also require difficult decisions as practitioners often have to balance the needs of the child for permanency and stability with potential for a match in terms of heritage and culture, and larger sibling groups may pose particular difficulties. In managing this complex set of imperatives it is important nevertheless, that children do not 'drift on' in insecure emergency placements that threaten their longer-term well-being and/or connection with their original family network.

Social workers are required to make practice judgements that consider both the needs of the child and the needs of the family, even though these may, at times, have conflicting interests. As Thoburn (1999: p. 140) observes:

> The art of child placement lies in being clear about what each family is looking for in terms of rewards and what they want and are able to give to the child; and matching them with a child who is likely to be able to give what they hope to receive, and to take from them what they hope to give.

Supporting placements and monitoring progress

Altruism may be a motivating factor for successful foster caregivers, but to truly succeed they need and seek support services. Furthermore, support services maximize retention, minimize agency costs, and prevent placement breakdown (Hek, 2010). Caregivers seek support that includes having available and reliable social workers who listen to, value, and respect and visit them frequently. Caregivers want to be included as part of a team, be involved in reviews, and be provided with information about the children in their care. They want more training, guidance regarding contact with parents, support when children leave their care, and access to respite care (Triseliotis et al., 2000: pp. 172–3). Carers are responding to the needs of children which may be complex and challenging, and therapeutic support that recognizes both the strain they are under and their experiences may also help with supporting the placement (Ironside, 2004; Hart and Lucklock, 2006).

A number of UK studies have explored the value and impact of training directly aimed at, and provided for, foster carers. Whilst the outcomes for the longer-term care of the child are mixed, overall carers valued the opportunities to access training and wanted to use the skills they developed. The mixed results of the longer-term effect of the various training programmes reflect the difficulties carers had in securing the time and support to implement their new skills, getting the ongoing social work support needed for their work with the child and the sustainability of the learning when the training programmes were relatively short (Allen and Vostanis, 2005; MacDonald and Turner, 2005; Herbert and Wookey, 2007).

For kinship carers, support from professionals is a complex experience. Research across international jurisdictions suggests that kinship
carers often receive limited support and despite policy guidance
may not be able to access the services they need (see for example,
Family Rights Group, 2009; Worrall, 2009; Higgins et al., 2007).
Farmer (2009a) from her study of children with kinship carers also
points to the higher levels of disadvantage experienced by kinship
carers and the very difficult task they undertake – with less support
than unrelated carers. Despite the reduced support and increased
challenges the evidence is that placement outcomes for children
with kinship carers and for children with unrelated carers may not
be significantly different (Hunt, 2008), suggesting kinship carers are
working very hard to maintain and support children, sometimes in
very difficult circumstances.

Despite the prevalence of out-of-home care, historically there has
been a lack of attention to the social worker's role once a child is placed
in care. As Calder and Horwath (2000: p. 268) note:

> There is an irony in that so much time, energy and resources are invested in
> following procedures up to and including the registration of the child on the
> child protection register, but once this has occurred guidance become hazy,
> with lack of literature regarding how we should be working with children and
> their carers.

Recent developments in research about foster care have increased
the social work knowledge base (Sellick, 2006), but attention is still
primarily focused on the early stages of interaction with children
needing protection and care. Support for children in the state
care system is an area of growing concern in some countries (see
for example the Care Matters programme developed by the UK
Government) but social work practice in this area requires further
support and development. The demands of child protection still
drive much social work practice with children and families, and
heightened public awareness about abuse can place further strain
on limited resources.

Different countries organize their statutory care support services in
care in different ways. Social workers in the UK have traditionally held
two distinct and separate roles. One social worker is responsible for
arranging the placement and supporting the family (placement or link
workers), the other is responsible for working directly with the child

(children's social workers). In their study, Triseliotis et al. (2000) found that while placement workers had a lower caseload than children's workers, both caseloads were considered 'too high' or 'unacceptably heavy'. Furthermore, role confusion and lack of opportunity for communication or collaboration can create tensions between placement and children's workers. Across Australia and New Zealand the support of children in statutory care and their carers is managed in a variety of ways. For example, in Victoria care is generally managed by the non-government sector. In New Zealand a mixed delivery of service is provided, sometimes by the state, and sometimes in partnership with non-government services. The nature of the service delivery then inevitably influences decisions with respect to who provides what support for the caregiver and the child.

In addition to providing support for the placement, part of the professional role is to assess and monitor the child's progress, and to help with this, several countries have developed mechanisms for such assessment. For example, in the UK, Looking After Children (LAC) materials were developed in response to concern about the quality of practice in foster care. It provides a means of ensuring the needs of children, particularly their developmental, health and educational needs, are identified and met (Clare, 1997; Moyers, 1995). The LAC records were considered a useful tool with the potential not only to maximize the benefits of out-of-home care and minimize the harm, but also to ensure consistency across agency practices and continuity in the care children receive. A number of countries adapted and implemented the records with minor changes required to fit different cultural contexts (for example, Canada, Sweden, and Australia).

More recently additional practice frameworks have emerged to assist with assessment and planning, such as the Framework for Assessment developed by the Government in the UK (DH, 2000) and the Integrated Children's System (DOH, 2000), the later seeking to bring together the Assessment Framework with the LAC material. The policy guidance and legal frameworks set out for local authorities in England and Wales have placed expectations for consistency and quality in planning for children who are looked after by the local authority. Not all these developments have been without their critics (Hall et al., 2010) and there are concerns that they narrow the capacity for responsive, skilled professional practice. These policy developments are, nevertheless, evidence of the general push towards effective management of children's time in the care system with the intention of securing better longer-term outcomes.

Contact and support of children in care

The central role families play in children's lives is increasingly recognized in social work practice with children in care (Sinclair, 2004). Contact between a child in care and their family has become an established part of the arrangements that social workers develop and review for children. Some forms of foster care present greater levels of activity surrounding contact – short-term fostering arrangements are more likely to include arrangements for children to maintain their connections with their family (Wilson, 2004), but the rushed nature of some emergency short-term arrangements may cause problems for planning contact.

Cleaver's study (2000) considered the contact experiences of families, foster carers and children in a number of English local authorities. They could identity a change in social work practice, with increased attention paid to contact following the implementation of the Children Act 1989. Carers could support and promote contact when they felt trained and equipped to do so, and children benefited from parental contact in terms of their behaviour and in any subsequent reunification process. But contact can also be challenging and at times problematic, requiring careful and considered practice and some groups such as adolescents may find the experiences of family contact particularly difficult (Moyers et al., 2006).

In discussing the social worker's role in determining the needs of children in care, Gilligan (2000a) suggests attention to detail will promote good outcomes for children. He argues that along with providing adequate practical resources, social workers can encourage and support children's contact with family, siblings and peers, educational and leisure activities, and nurture their talents. In this way, social workers can enhance the child's competence and confidence and optimize opportunities for them to develop resilience. A social worker's commitment will help a child to feel they 'matter' and that they 'count'. Social workers need to focus on, 'what can sustain the positive development of the child today ... . A focus on longer-term planning may obscure helpful practical things that can be done now – and thus make the child's problems and long-term planning for them more difficult' (p. 123).

> **KEY PRACTICE QUESTIONS 6.1**
>
> 1. What are the differences between prospective kin and non-kin caregivers and how might these differences influence caregiver assessment processes?
> 2. How might the need for an emergency placement influence placement decisions?
> 3. Given the particular support needs of new placements, what might a practitioner do to help sustain them?

Practice partnerships

To work effectively in this complex and demanding field, workers need to establish good relationships with children, their families, foster caregivers, and other professionals and agencies.

Partnerships with families

As removing children from their homes is generally a temporary measure, establishing good relationships with parents/caregivers is vital in terms of assessing the ability of the parent to ensure the child's safety once returned home. Bullock et al. (1993) established that 92 per cent of children in the care system in England and Wales would return home at some point – indicating the importance of family involvement. Concerns remain about the extent and nature of family participation in planning for children and there is limited evidence of significant change in levels of social work engagement with families (Wilson et al., 2004). Christie and Mittler (1999), however, remind us that the relationship between professionals and parents/caregivers is not one of equality. Professionals have expertise and access to a common language that places parents and caregivers at a disadvantage. On the other hand, the limited knowledge professionals have of the social world of children and their families, means families have the expertise to more accurately assess the risks and contribute to a more informed decision-making process.

A constructive relationship with family members involves an attitude of respect and liking for the primary carer, an understanding of their point of view, and the ability to establish common ground upon which to base an intervention plan that addresses the carer's needs as well as the child's. Yet demands upon the social work process can come at the expense of responding to the needs of parents or caregivers who are struggling to cope with an alien and traumatic experience. When the parent/caregiver's need for help and understanding is ignored this will have an impact on the level of support they are able to offer the child (Farmer and Owen, 1995). Even where alienation has occurred, however, carers who want to be 'more involved in decision making... respond to skilled and sensitive workers' with positive results (Morrison, 1996: p. 132). Kapp and Propp (2002) suggest that effective communication is important and this echoes the earlier findings of Bullock et al. (1993) who suggest inclusive social work practice is particularly important in supporting family involvement, and can be linked to a later successful return home of a child.

New Zealand's FGC model clearly demonstrates that positive results can be achieved by strengthening the family network and enhancing the family's commitment to outcomes. By sharing the responsibility for the child's protection with the family, professionals have the potential to increase 'the safety net for children at risk' (Connolly, 1999: p. 33). Where the child is in alternative care, the FGC is used for review purposes, which, in turn, 'enables the child to re-establish links with the original family, and for the original family and the foster family to work together in the best interest of the child' (p. 126).

Whilst most studies highlight the advantages of working in partnership with families, particularly where clients are self-motivated, they also indicate that partnerships are difficult to form with families who may prefer not to receive services, and who remain defensive, or even hostile. Ferguson (2010) suggests that greater recognition needs to be given to the fact that the threat or risk of violence can undermine the ability of social workers to form relationships with families. Furthermore, the realities of child protection practice are not always acknowledged, while training does not adequately prepare graduates for working in the field – something that raised particular concerns for the Social Work Reform Board created by the UK Government to address widespread concern regarding the training and role of social workers.

Partnership with caregivers

Given the number of children who live in foster homes and the difficult and complex work caregivers are called to do, partnerships with foster caregivers needs to be a high priority for practitioners. Yet lack of agency support, poor communication, lack of information, lack of involvement in decision-making, plans and reviews are cited as reasons for foster caregivers withdrawing from fostering. The fact that the partnership between social workers and foster caregivers tends to vary in quality, may be reflected in the uneasy relationship that exists between them. Selwyn and Quinton (2004) found that levels of social work support received by long-term foster carers were often basic and that carers had great difficulty accessing extra or specialist support. Foster caregivers are often reluctant to ask for help in case they are perceived as 'unable to cope', whilst social workers are reluctant to intervene, 'with people … who might be much more experienced in child care than themselves' (Berridge, 1997: pp. 72–3).

Morgan (2005) found that foster carers identified having an accessible supportive link to social workers to be the most valuable support, but that carers still felt they had inadequate information about the children they were looking after, and felt they had had insufficient training. Sargent and O'Brien (2004) found that carers wanted to be valued for their skills and knowledge and consulted about the children they looked after, and overall the evidence suggests that this type of respect for carer's expertise is a prerequisite for working in partnership with foster carers.

An environment of respect and trust has also been identified as important, particularly in the context of supporting Indigenous caregivers, as Higgins et al. (2007: p. 4) note from an Australian perspective:

> A major issue identified for nearly all carers … was relationships with
> child protection department workers. … Even when carers were receiving
> direct support from a non-government agency, they still felt the need for
> a more supportive relationship with the child's caseworker in particular,
> and the department generally. The relationship was further strained
> between Indigenous agencies, carers and the department due to carers
> feeling that the department mistrusts Aboriginal and Torres Strait Islander
> communities.

Professional and agency collaboration

Interdisciplinary work is an increasing feature of contemporary social work practice, in part in recognition of the need to develop holistic approaches to children's needs (Morris et al., 2009). Recent developments in supporting the care of children away from their families have reflected this shift towards collaborative working. McDonald et al. (2003) examined an interdisciplinary support project for carers involving health, social services and education which sought to offer an integrated service with access for carers to interdisciplinary consultation and direct support to carers and children. Although a small scale study, its findings suggest some interesting developments: the carers felt that the intervention provided by the support team had focused on them rather than the child and they saw this as a positive development in helping them meet the child's needs. By offering inter-disciplinary support, carers could access services and support from a full range of agencies and so could more readily respond appropriately to the needs of the child. But carers wanted to be an acknowledged partner in the multi-agency team – and to have their roles valued and respected. Likewise, Golding (2004) found that easy access to relevant services and being acknowledged as part of an expert team were positive benefits of multi-agency support teams for carers. Overall the evidence is positive about the potential of collaborative working in supporting the carers of children, and ultimately such developments can be argued to reflect the complex and demanding role carers are increasingly expected to fulfil.

Conclusion

Foster and kinship care are now the most utilized options for children requiring out-of-home care. In this chapter we have noted the unique differences between these two types of care, and the differing needs of caregivers. Recognizing these differences and developing more responsive policy and practice has the potential to better support placements and ultimately to support good outcomes for children at risk.

FURTHER READING

Adoption & Fostering, a British journal dedicated to developments in care, including supports for caregivers. See http://www.baaf.org.uk/res/pubs/aandf/about/.

Argent, H. (2006) *Top Ten Tips for Placing Children in Permanent Families*, London: British Association for Adopting and Fostering.

Farmer, E. and Moyers, S. (2008) *Kinship Care: Fostering Effective Family and Friends Placements*, London: Jessica Kingsley Publishers.

USEFUL WEBSITES

The Australian Foster Care Association represents the voices of foster carers throughout Australia. Their website is retrievable at: http://www.fostercare.org.au/index.html.

The Fostering Network is a UK charity aiming to provide support for anyone with a personal or professional involvement in fostering. Their website is retrievable at http://www.fostering.net.

The New Zealand Family and Foster Care Federation's aim is to provide quality support to carers of children in out-of-home care. Their website is retrievable at: http://www.fostercarefederation.org.nz/about_us.

7

The experiences and voices of children in care

> **Key Points**
>
> - Whilst there is a significant body of research and practice literature relating to children and care, it is important that we explore this from the perspective of the child.
> - Involving children and young people in decision-making processes can make a positive difference to the way they experience out-of-home care.
> - In recent years there has been a significant shift in perceptions towards recognizing children's rights to both safety and nurturing care over time.

Children can provide crucial information about their experiences of being in care. They can also provide advice on how we interpret what they say. This is critical to how we understand systems of care, and if we want to improve them, we need to ask children and young people to share their insights with us. In this chapter we will look at the experiences of children who receive care and protection services. There is a growing body of research exploring the experiences of children and young people, and increasingly attention is being paid to the rights of children to have their voices heard, and their views acknowledged. It is this body of research that will be our primary focus in this chapter.

As we have noted in previous chapters there has been growing interest in the experiences of, and outcomes for, children involved with care and protection systems. Internationally comparisons of children's experiences have been made (Thoburn, 2007) and caution expressed about the exchange of evidence of effective interventions without understanding the contextual issues and their implications. Alongside this developing literature concerned with child welfare outcomes research has emerged that seeks to reveal the lived experiences of children who are the subject of care and protection interventions. This chapter brings together these two strands to consider how children experience care and protection services and the skills that practitioners need to develop to respond to the needs of children and young people. All children do not have the same shared experiences – some groups of children experience specific barriers and difficulties. Indigenous children, often over-represented in statutory care systems, ethnic minority children, refugee and asylum seeking children, and disabled children face additional challenges in accessing safe, effective care. For some groups of children, little is known about their wishes and well-being. For example, Hek (2007) points to the limited information about unaccompanied asylum seeking children's views and experiences of fostering and others have also identified the need to expand our knowledge of marginalized groups of children (Connolly et al., 2008). Assumptions cannot therefore be made about children's experiences and views, and this reinforces the need for responsive, culturally sensitive social work practice.

Research from the child's perspective

Over the past decade, two themes in particular have emerged strongly in research related to children. Firstly, a growing interest in exploring children's experience through direct research with children. This has required the development of appropriate research tools and has presented traditional approaches to research with a number of challenges both ethically and methodologically (Christensen and James, 2008; Greig et al., 2007; Alderson and Morrow, 2004). As Curtis et al. (2004) suggest, marginalized children still are under-represented in the research and accessing and researching with excluded and marginalized groups of children requires new and innovative approaches. Secondly, there has been a growth in participative research – where children are not just the subject of attention but also play an active role in designing the research and gathering the data (Alderson, 2001). These two strands of activity require different understandings of the role and rights of children, but both offer important insights into children's experiences. As Coad and Lewis (2004: p. 48) suggest:

> We have stressed that children are a primary source about their own views and experiences and must be therefore listened to. However... engaging children in research raises particular challenges and concerns. Thus, there is a need to carefully consider such issues if research with children and young people is to be taken seriously.

In child welfare, early research generally focused on retrospective studies. More recent research has explored the experiences of children currently in care. Several themes emerge from these studies including: the children's vulnerability; health; their educational attainment; their participation and consultation in the decision-making process; their level of satisfaction with their experiences of being in care; and their contact with their biological families. Indeed Berridge (1997; 2005) and Sinclair (2005) suggest that studies revealing children's experiences are important contributions to practice development and that children's views need to be seen as a key indicator of successful and good quality foster placements.

The development in the UK of the 'Every Child Matters' programme for change identified five outcomes that services for children need to pay attention to: staying safe, being healthy, educational achievement, making a positive contribution and economic well-being. Given the complexities of children's needs and experiences, these five dimensions of children's well-being present real challenges for those supporting children entering and staying in the public care systems (DCSF, 2006). They reflect, nevertheless, a shift towards understandings of 'well-being' as opposed to restricted perspectives on specific aspects of a child's care pathway. This expanded understanding of children's needs and experiences has led to significant UK policy and service developments for children in care (DCSF, 2006), and a shift in perceptions towards recognizing children's rights to both safety and nurturing care over time.

Vulnerability

Children come into care at all ages – from birth to adolescence. An overall picture of children who come into care reveals that they are likely to have a background of disadvantage and poverty, maltreatment, abuse and neglect, poor physical health, developmental delays, psychological and behavioural problems, and low educational attainment. The caregivers for these children will often confront difficult issues and will require considerable skill if they are to be successful in their caregiving (Sinclair, 2004, Wilson, 2004). The safety of children in care is a complex area of practice, as McLeod (2010) recognizes in her study of children's feelings towards social workers – children want practitioners to be a friend and an equal. She suggests that in exploring these views from children it is possible to see how social workers can develop professional practice that both meets their professional and legal obligations and the needs of the child. Her research does, nevertheless, reveal the complex role social workers play in responding to the needs of the most vulnerable of children.

There are ongoing concerns about stability for children in care (Sinclair, 2010a; Ward, 2008) and an acknowledgement that it remains a challenge to understand and address. Frequent placement moves increases children's vulnerability and can significantly impact their emotional development and well-being. The statistics relating to placement moves, however, may not always reflect children's realities. Some short-term moves for children may be planned, such as a return home after a limited time in care. Equally some children may remain long-term in a placement (thereby indicating positive stability) but actually may be receiving poor care and inadequate future planning. Sinclair (2010b) suggests that the key to good outcomes is to maintain a focus that ensures children are sustained in the *right* placement and that this can be achieved through the increased use of kinship care, adoption or genuinely supported placements that provide a home for life. He argues that developing good quality assurance for placements and helping social workers become committed to best practice will positively support good outcomes for children. Again, this indicates the key role that social workers can play in promoting positive outcomes for children in care.

The Children's Rights Director of England (Morgan, 2005) gathered together the views of children in care about their social workers. Children articulated what they found helpful and unhelpful and what they saw to be the qualities of a good social worker. The findings included ease of access, being child rather than adult focused, helping before a crisis developed and giving any help promised quickly. Conversely children felt social workers were unhelpful when they listen to the adults rather than the child, were restrictive and set rules that aimed to minimize risk rather than meet the child's needs and when they failed to do what they had promised. Hek et al. (2010), in their review of the literature, suggest that children often rated their foster carers as being highly important people in their lives. Indeed, for those in longer-term placements carers were often rated as more important than birth parents. Children in care, however, identified a common sense of 'not belonging' and feeling different. These feelings were heightened by the number of people involved in their lives, the meetings that had to be held, difference in surnames with a foster family, and social workers not listening to what they had to say. In a UK kinship care study, frequent changes in social worker undermined the children's confidence in them:

> I get used to one social worker and confide in them, and then they say they are going. One I met once. (Doolan et al., 2004: p. 39)

Timms and Thoburn (2003) asked children in the public care system in the UK a series of questions about their experiences and views. Common themes could be identified – many of which have direct implications for child welfare practice and for the vulnerability of children in the care system. The responses to their survey indicated that a significant number of children did not know the name of the Local Authority responsible for their well-being, and over a quarter did not know their care plan – most worryingly one in five of the children that responded did not feel that being in care made them feel safer.

Whilst policy and practice may have moved on and attention to the needs of children in public care systems has developed, some experiences for children remain difficult and distressing. In studies children repeatedly ask that they are not treated differently, and that they should have the same experiences as any children in their placement who are not fostered (Morgan, 2005). For example, in a recent UK care review children saw the continued use of plastic bags to transport their possessions as indicative of a lack of care (DCSF, 2010a).

Positive aspects of foster care for children include the feeling of being loved, cared for and supported, having someone who will listen and understand them, feeling they belong, that they fit in and are 'part of the family'. Selwyn et al. (2008) interviewed children and young people about their views on being cared for by an independent foster care provider. Overall most of the children and young people expressed high levels of satisfaction with their care and the majority of children felt secure and trusted their carers. Children do, nevertheless, have ambivalent views of being in care. Aldgate and Bradley (1999) found that children in short-term care were homesick and concerned about being rejected and not being able to return home. Towards the end of placements, however, the majority of children were positive about their experience and the care they had received. Several studies indicate that while children feel that being in a foster home is the best thing for them and that their quality of life has improved, they also miss their biological families and ideally want to live with them (Fox et al., 2000; Sinclair et al., 2001).

Studies also indicate a high degree of satisfaction with kinship care, which is generally less disruptive than stranger foster care in terms of established social relationships and interaction. Hunt's study (2008) points to the difficulties in comparing kinship care experiences with those of unrelated caregiving placements. There are complex issues facing kinship carers including poverty, difficult family relationships and poor support (FRG, 2009). Hunt's research suggests that children in kinship care placements experienced their care as positive with responses indicating high levels of security and trust in their carer. And Broad's study also suggests that kinship care offers children important opportunities for safe and positive care (Broad, 2004).

In an analysis of Australian research into out-of-home care Bromfield and her colleagues (2005) found that overall most children and young people in care were broadly positive about their experiences, considering their foster homes to be secure and supportive. In general they also saw their workers as helpful and willing to listen. The majority, nevertheless, wanted increased contact and connection with their families of origin. Having a trusted and stable relationship with one person was also seen as of critical importance. Whilst the findings from the analysis were positive overall, children and young people did however, experience instances of poor practice. In the overall scheme of things, oversights that may not be considered important to the worker were acutely felt by the children, compounding feelings of sadness, loss and their sense of being different. In the context of placement breakdown, poor practice, including poor communication and consultation, were identified by the children as having a negative impact on placement sustainability.

Clearly, this summary of some of the findings from research with children in care indicates that social workers need to focus attention on listening to children, developing effective communication skills, ensuring children are kept fully informed of their arrangements and making certain children can access safe, appropriate help. Social workers play an important role in the lives of children in out-of-home care, and the impact of poor practice cannot be underestimated.

Education

Educational experiences and outcomes for children in care have direct links into their overall well-being and life outcomes once they leave the care systems. Historically children in care have had poor educational outcomes (Zetlin et al., 2005), but their learning needs have nevertheless received limited attention. Jackson and Sachdev (2001) suggest that over 70 per cent of children in foster care and 80 per cent of children in residential care in the UK left school without qualifications, with very few progressing on to further or higher education. Children in care were also ten times more likely to be excluded from school. This picture of children failing to achieve and becoming disconnected from the education systems led to considerable concern in the UK, in part driven by concerns about later outcomes in life, including unemployment and antisocial behaviour. The research by Jackson and Sachdev included asking children in care about their experiences of education. They described receiving limited support for their education, disruption in their schooling when placement moves occur; low aspirations and expectations and difficulties caused by limited inter-agency communication and working. Martin and Jackson (2002) explored the experiences of children who had been in care and who had succeeded at school – in so doing they sought to identify the approaches that were experienced as helpful. The responses stressed the importance of being 'normal' and the same as other people in their day-to-day lives. Over a third of the participants felt that there was a process of labelling and stereotyping of children in care and that this meant that teachers had low expectations of them and expected them to be disruptive. Whilst identifying the careful care and attention needed by children in care to succeed at school, there was also a strong sense that they should not be marked out as different by service providers and professionals.

A review of the research conducted in the UK a decade on from the initial policy drive to raise the profile of the educational needs of children in care suggests that the policy and practice attention given to education for children in care has resulted in positive benefits. Children now see entering care as having positive effects on their education and a variety of initiatives to address the learning needs of children in care appear to have improved educational outcomes (Brodie, 2009). But it is evident that attention needs to be paid to all stages of education and that measuring outcomes is complex, as education outcomes are closely linked to the other events in children's lives (Sinclair, 2004; Farmer et al., 2004). There are gaps in the evidence base and the challenges of understanding educational outcomes which may or may not be directly linked to other, allied developments in a child's life are many. Brodie's review is clear that children in the public care system are children first, and school plays an important part in their lives as it does for all children. Children in care continue to place importance on their schooling, as Sinclair (2005: p. 97) notes: 'school featured prominently in children's accounts of what was important in placements'.

The role of social workers and carers in promoting better education outcomes is also apparent in the research (Brodie, 2009; Sinclair, 2005). Carers and social workers need to work carefully with children to support their learning. This may go beyond simple school attendance and needs to take notice of children's wishes and needs (Martin and Jackson, 2002). Sinclair (2004) suggests a broad view of schooling should be adopted, and the happiness of a child at school deserves consideration alongside their educational attainments.

Health

Increasingly studies have been able to explore the risk factors that are linked to long-term poor outcomes for vulnerable children, and also the protective factors that seem to help some children survive adversity and develop resilience. But, as France et al. (2010) and Biehal (2008) both suggest, we still need to know a great deal more about how risk and protective factors interact and lead to particular outcomes for children. Indeed, France argues the focus has been largely upon risk factors and our understanding of preventive, protective factors is less well developed. As a result interventions that seek to promote children's resilience and to help them cope with the complex experiences of entering and remaining in public care require further examination and development. Studies repeatedly identify the high levels of problems experienced by children before they enter the care systems: figures for England suggest that over 60 per cent of children who enter the care system have been the subject of abuse and/or neglect (DCSF, 2009). Once they are within the care system the evidence is that they have higher levels of need, including attachment difficulties and that this impacts upon their experiences of, and responses to, the care that they are offered.

The mental health of looked after children has been the subject of a number of studies (Halfon et al., 2002; Richardson and Joughlin, 2002; Park and Ryan, 2009). Research indicates that children in care have significantly higher rates of mental health disorders than children brought up in their own families (Bromfield et al., 2005; Meltzer et al., 2003). Children present with complex needs, including 'conduct problems and defiance, attachment insecurity and disturbance, attention-deficit/hyperactivity, trauma related anxiety and sexual behaviour' (Bromfield et al., 2005: p. 34).

Historically the physical health of children in care has received very little research attention despite evidence that children in care experience significant health problems (Meltzer et al., 2003; Takayama et al., 1998; Nathanson and Tzioumi, 2007). Children come into care with a range of acute and chronic illnesses and physical abnormalities and require access to health care services. As the National Children's Bureau notes, however, limited research has been developed that specifically looks at the health needs and care of children in the care system (NCB, 2010). The broader picture in the UK of poor health in children (driven by increased obesity, dietary problems and lack of exercise) raises specific concerns for the children within the care system. The UK Government Care Matters programme has therefore begun to address the health care of children in care suggesting they have a right to:

- experience a genuinely caring, supportive, stable and secure relationship with at least one committed, trained, experienced and supported carer
- live in an environment that promotes health and well-being within the wider community
- have opportunities to develop personal and social skills to care for their health and well-being now and in the future
- receive effective health care, assessment, treatment and support.

(DCSF, 2010b)

As a consequence of the high levels of complex needs being identified, a diverse range of projects and schemes have been developed with the aim of offering support to children in care in order to promote better outcomes for them. Ways of better assessing and responding to the health and education needs of out-of-home children in New Zealand have been identified (Rankin and Mills, 2008), and Australian initiatives to improve the safety and well-being of children in out-of-home care have been developed (see for example, State of Victoria, 2001).

KEY PRACTICE QUESTIONS 7.1

1. How might entry into care increase a child's vulnerability?
2. Why do children's educational experiences impact on a child's life outcomes?
3. How might a lack of information about a child's health needs impact on their experience in out-of-home care?

Children's participation

The growing body of research and literature exploring children's participation in decision-making makes it also possible to explore children's experiences of involvement in the decisions that affect their lives and choices. Consistent with the expectations of the United Nations Convention on the Rights of the Child (UNCROC) there are policy expectations that children are consulted about plans for their wellbeing. For example, in England the Children and Young Persons Act 2008 led to guidance for those reviewing children's care plans that included clear expectations of consultation with the child. Such developments have aimed to ensure that children no longer feel excluded from care planning and their wishes and knowledge are included in the planning process (DCSF, 2010b). Countries that have developed family decision-making models of practice also support the greater involvement and participation of children in matters relating to their care (Connolly, 1999).

The development of family decision-making in care and protection has opened up opportunities for children's participation in decisions that are made about their lives. Several studies make the point that attendance is not necessarily participation and that being listened to is not the same as being influential (Sieppert and Unrau, 2003). These studies suggest that specific skills are needed to ensure that children's views are part of the process. They also indicate, nevertheless, that children did feel that they had their say, and that family decision-making processes were preferred to professional processes (Laws and Kirby, 2007; Holland et al., 2006).

The influence of previous practices, where children were not invited to be part of the decision-making process, tends to blur the distinction between children expressing their views and asking for what they want (Cashmore and O'Brien, 2001; Munro, 2001). While legislation encourages children's participation in decision-making, messages from the research suggest that children do not feel their views are invited, accepted, or respected. Yet even being listened to helps, as this young person indicates:

> There is a person called A who lives up the road, she is a big part of my life, because she sits down and talks and I can let things out.... I can let more things out with A – she listens, not many people do that. Not many people listen to what I have got to say. (Thomas and O'Kane, 2000: p. 831)

In a study of kinship care, Doolan and his colleagues (2004) examined the views of 37 British children who responded to their survey, and 11 children who agreed to be interviewed. The children indicated the need for them to be more knowledgeable about what was happening, and more involved in the decisions made about them:

> [The social worker] came round in secret and saw my aunt and uncle. My cousin told me she had been and she had told them I had been depressed and wanted to be with Mum. I was worried I might get kicked out. She got hold of the wrong end of the stick...

> I can't do anything without the social worker knowing. To go and stay with friends they need to have six weeks notice. I'm embarrassed about having them police checked. (Doolan et al., 2004: pp. 40–42)

Children, particularly those who have experienced abuse, value participation in discussions about what is to happen to them and are more likely to accept the outcomes when they are involved. Morgan's (2005) analysis of the views of children who have been fostered found common messages from children and young people about the need for adequate consultation and information, good consistent levels of support and the need to experience genuine efforts to ensure they did not feel excluded or the 'odd one out'. Foster carers, teachers and social workers were seen as having important roles to play in these processes.

That children want opportunities to participate in their care is clearly evident. In their review of children's views of services, Mainey and colleagues (2008: p. 19) suggest:

> There is a strong message from all areas of children's services that children and young people want to be involved in the planning and delivery of the services they receive.

Children want to be involved in choosing their placement and have a greater say in the development of their care plans and how the plans are implemented (Morgan, 2005; Timms and Thoburn, 2003). That is not to say that children will necessarily find involvement easy. They may want or need support to be able to contribute – they may not understand the processes or the language used. It is important, therefore, to be creative in finding ways to enhance their contribution. The use of advocates for children is a developing practice, and a number of the studies have explored advocacy practice skills needed to ensure children's participation is supported (Sieppert and Unrau, 2003; Holland and O'Neill, 2006).

Article 12 of the United Nations Convention on the Rights of the Child (UNCROC) clearly expects children to be actively consulted in matters that concern them:

> State parties shall assure to the child who is capable of forming his or her own views the right to express those views freely in all matters affecting the child, the views of the child being given due weight in accordance with the age and maturity of the child.

State parties that have ratified UNCROC, therefore, need to consider ways in which they can give effect to these expectations in law, policy and practice (Connolly and Ward, 2008).

KEY PRACTICE QUESTIONS 7.2

1. How can laws and policies reflect a greater commitment to children's participation?
2. How can children be supported to participate?
3. What tensions are there in supporting a children's rights perspective in practice?

Contact with families

Studies reveal the importance of maintaining contact between children and their families of origin. In general, children want more contact with their families and spend a great deal of time thinking about them (Cleaver, 2000; Wilson et al., 2004). For children who have no contact at all with their parents, contact with extended family can be particularly important. Social workers and carers play a key role in supporting contact and Wilson's research found that poor practice and unnecessary difficulties in supporting arrangements for contact meant at times children did not have the level of contact expected. The evidence indicates that children may have a more successful return to home and their mental health may be better supported if contact arrangements are carefully maintained (Sinclair, 2005). Clarity is needed about the meaning of contact: it may simply involve occasionally letters or reports, but it may involve intense, frequent visits. There is a need for careful social work practice that distinguishes the different contact needs a child may have in relation to different family members.

All the research reveals the importance of contact, and, as Sinclair identifies, attention by policy makers and professionals to contact for children in public care has increased. There are still real challenges for social workers and carers, nevertheless, in supporting contact arrangements. There are practical considerations about costs – for example, travel costs for birth parents can put strain on family budgets. Geography also plays a part, in that practical arrangements for contact when the child and their family are distanced from each other needs careful consideration (Sinclair, 2004). Often busy social workers and carers may not prioritize contact arrangements, and whilst this may be a simple reflection of the demands on their time, it may also reveal some instinctive responses to birth families if their care has been found to be poor or neglectful. The value of maintaining family connections for a child, however, can be considerable and their emotional well-being and their psychological developmental needs are usually better supported where contact is maintained (Wilson, 2004; Cleaver, 2004). As Fox, Frasch and Berrick (2000: p. 81) note, 'continuity with birth parents provides children with the necessary knowledge that they have not been abandoned. In turn, this knowledge allows children to trust and develop distinctive relationships with new substitute caregivers'.

Immediate family members, usually mothers, are the most common focus for contact but also siblings, aunts, uncles and grandparents are important. For some groups of children contact can be a complex experience. Farmer's study of adolescents and contact suggests that whilst young people may be more able to independently develop contact arrangements, they also can experience higher levels of difficult and potentially harmful contact (Farmer et al., 2004).

Contact with family, however, is not always possible (particularly if a parent is either dead or missing), or appropriate (where the history of abuse or conflict between the child and the parent is enduringly harmful for the child). These situations are unusual – only a minority of children have no contact at all with their birth family (Sinclair, 2004; Cleaver, 2002). Sinclair suggests that practice with these children could be strengthened to ensure that these isolated young people can be supported and their needs addressed (2005).

Broad's study of kinship care echoes the general trend in such studies, namely that placement with family and friends can make contact an easier and less artificial process (Broad, 2004). There are, however, challenges for kinship carers in supporting family contact, not least when the reasons for providing kinship care are rooted in the inappropriate care previously provided by parents. Kroll (2007) identifies the particular challenges facing kinship care placements where the parents are unable to look after their children because of substance misuse. Whilst family placements, in particular placements with grandparents, are important positive opportunities for children, there can be very difficult family dynamics to confront which require skilled professional input. This reinforces Broad's wider point that supporting kinship care is a challenging task for professionals, requiring the development of skills in mediation, relationship based practice and cross-cultural competency that previous placements practices may not have necessitated.

Contact with siblings plays an important part in maintaining continuity and identity, and can also be a source of support and reassurance for children in care. Siblings 'may be the only people who come close to grasping the reality of life in their common family of origin' and provide the basis for life-long 'commitment and support' (Gilligan, 2000b: p. 143). As children in out-of-home care are likely to have siblings who are also in the system (Shlonsky, Webster & Needell, 2003), the need to place siblings together is recognized in legislation across a number of countries. Siblings are more likely to be placed together when they start care at the same time, are placed with relatives, and are of the same gender. A Scottish study (Triseliotis et al., 2000) revealed that 22 per cent of caregivers were fostering a sibling group, usually involving two children. There are times, of course, when it is not appropriate or possible for siblings to be placed together, for example, when a sibling relationship is abusive (Whelan, 2003).

Leaving care

Schofield and Beek (2005) emphasize the importance of building resilience characteristics such as self-esteem, the capacity to seek help and cope alone, the capacity to reflect, and so on. They draw on their own previous studies to show that good long-term carers naturally build on these abilities throughout childhood (Beek and Schofield, 2004). They also found that internal resilience features are often strengthened via good networks outside of the carer's family. They link this ability to have outside positive networks with the idea of having good 'social capital'. Young adults who have been through foster care report that wider networks are extremely valuable to them on leaving care, particularly when the networks are also valued by their carers (Schofield, 2003). Research, nevertheless suggests that for many young people who have been in care the longer-term outcomes are poor, and economic well-being is difficult to achieve. Children who have been in care are over-represented in those young adults experiencing homelessness, mental health difficulties, teenage pregnancies and committing crime (Stein, 2002; 2004; Dixon et al., 2007). Such experiences are connected with long-term poor outcomes and make stable long-term economic well-being for young people leaving care a difficult target for services to achieve.

For children, the age at which they came into care, the length of time they have been in care, and the circumstances that have precipitated the move will determine how they manage the process of leaving care. Grieving will be less intense where the move is planned and expected than when it occurs suddenly (Edelstein, Burge and Waterman, 2001). For most children, leaving care is a planned process, and they are either reunified with their families, adopted, or they age out of care. A number of children who leave care, however, re-enter the care system at a later stage.

As before, it is important to recognize the different experiences that different groups of young people may have. Ince (1998) considered the experiences of black and minority ethnic care leavers and found many of the young people did not feel they received enough input from social workers or carers about their cultural or ethnic identity during their time in placement. Those who had been placed transracially questioned this placement decision, feeling that if they had been placed with black carers this may have been better for them. Most of the young people said they were not listened to about what they wanted from their placements. The overarching message from this study was one of engagement: placements worked best for children and young people when they were consulted by their social workers and carers at each step about their wishes and needs.

Family reunification

Returning children to their families after short-term placements shifts the focus from the child to the context of the family (Ainsworth, 1997). As a result, rather than providing substitute parenting, services are directed towards supporting the family and facilitating the child's eventual return home. As Wilson's review of the literature indicates, short-term foster care is valued by parents and by children (although they may initially be unhappy with the move from home) and the return home is often the focus of the interventions (Wilson et al., 2004).

The success of reunification depends on collaboration between all those directly involved in the child's care, programmed visits and parental involvement in the out-of-home care of the child, the emotional readiness of parents for reunification, preparation of the child for re-entry into the family, and the strength and intensity of formal and informal services both during placement and after reunification. Additional services and support are also needed, particularly education and training programmes that address parenting functioning. Where reunification is a valid goal, returning home needs to be part of the planning process throughout the child's time in care. Research has long established the valuable role that social workers play in successful reunification and the need for professional practice to adopt an inclusionary approach to work with the child and family (Bullock, 1993).

The outcomes for children returning home from care are the subject of a growing body of international research and literature. The majority of children will return home, but the age of the child, the reason they entered the public care system and the quality and type of support they receive all influence the possibilities for a successful and safe return home. Children in short-term care usually return home (Aldgate, 1999) whereas older children may well move towards living independently rather then returning to their families. However, it is evident that social work practice has a critical role to play in assessing and supporting the possibilities of reunification. Without careful planning children may be placed at further risk (Cleaver, 2000) but also without responsive practice that understands the changes that families and children experience reunification possibilities may be missed. Less is known about the experiences and views of children and their families once a child is returned home. Malet et al's study (2010) suggests that parents need considerable support and skilled services if they are to be able to overcome previous difficulties and experiences. Sinclair suggests that there are considerable gaps in our understandings of children's return home, particularly those children who have only stayed a short time in care (Sinclair, 2005). The poor outcomes for children who remain in the care system creates a complex context for understanding the outcomes for children reunified with their families. The failure to offer children and their carers (foster, birth or unrelated) effective support is a common theme across the piece and a key message is the need to develop skilled social work practices.

Adolescents aging out of care

Young people leaving care are a vulnerable group. Research in the UK by the Department of Health (1999) showed that care leavers were significantly less likely to be in work, education or training than their peer groups and were vulnerable in many areas of their lives.

In order to cope with the transition into adulthood, adolescents need, 'a sense of competence', connections (to family, caring adults and peers), and control over their lives; success is related to being able to make choices regarding their future (Williams, 2001: p. 5). Yet expecting adolescents between the ages of 16 and 18 to be socially, economically, and emotionally independent (Department of Health, 1996; Williams, 2001) is a high expectation given that comparatively few young people from stable homes are fully self-sufficient below the age of 21 (Mech, 2001). Expecting young people, whose lives have been disrupted, to reach independence ahead of their peers in normal families is, therefore, unrealistic. As Stein (2005: p. 1) suggests:

> For the majority of young people today their journey to adulthood often extends into their mid-twenties. It is a journey from restricted to full citizenship, from a childhood status characterised by dependency to an adult status derived in part on choices, such as becoming a student, employee, householder, partner and parent. But not all young people take the same path. Such life-course choices, from which adult rights and responsibilities flow, are mediated by the impact of their socio-economic background, their ethnicity, their gender and any disability they may have. In contrast to the extended transitions made by most young people, the journey to adulthood for many young care leavers is shorter, steeper and often more hazardous. And yet, against many odds, some of these young people have succeeded.

Issues of stability are linked to the outcomes for young people, multiple placement moves make it difficult for children to develop strong attachments and the support networks that can assist with the transition from care. Allen's 2003 study of young care leavers showed that if they were previously within a stable placement, they were more able to engage with opportunities for work, education and less likely to run the risk of isolation and poor outcomes. This study also showed that young people value both informal and formal support and demonstrated considerable resilience in their ongoing determination to build a positive future. For groups already vulnerable because of social disadvantage and isolation, such as refugee and asylum seeking children and black and minority ethnic children, the opportunities to build and use supportive networks are further limited by turbulent care careers (Barn, 2005, National Evaluation of the Children's Fund (NECF)).

Given the disadvantages faced by young people leaving care, several countries have introduced legislation to provide programmes to assist care leavers. The UK government introduced the Children (Leaving Care) Act 2000 setting out the duties to care for and support young people, and alongside the legislation a series of good practice guides were introduced looking at specific needs such as education, training and financial support (DH, 2002; DCSF, 2010b). Whilst these developments cannot remedy any prior shortcomings in children's experiences of care they have sought to focus attention on the years of transition for young people leaving care. Allard's (2002) study exploring the implementation of the legislation requiring support to be offered to care leavers suggests the intentions of the Act are limited by the previous experiences of children. So, whilst the Act may seek to promote opportunities for education and training, this may be frustrated by past experiences of insecure placements, poor education and interrupted care.

KEY PRACTICE QUESTIONS 7.3

1. What do practitioners need to know to provide effective care services for children?
2. What are some of the dilemmas facing social workers in supporting children in care?
3. How can practitioners best support children's pathway out of care?

Conclusion

Involving children and young people in the decision-making process can make a positive contribution to their experiences of out-of-home care and benefit their growth and development in the longer-term. A persistent theme throughout the literature is the need for better access to information and better communication between caregivers and children, caregivers and parents, caregivers and social service professionals, and children and practitioners. Listening to the voices of children who are, or have been, in care is critical if we are to provide responsive services that meet their needs.

FURTHER READING

Australian Children's Commissioners and Children's Guardians (2009) *How Australian Kids See The World: Commemorating 20 Years of the UN Convention on the Rights of the Child*, Sydney: New South Wales Government.

Joseph Rowntree Foundation (2005) *The Experiences of Young Care Leavers from Different Ethnic Groups*, available from http://www.jrf.org.uk/publications/experiences-young-care-leavers-different-ethnic-groups.

USEFUL WEBSITES

The Create Foundation is the peak body representing the voices of Australian children and young people in out-of-home care: http://www.create.org.au/about-us. The official website for the New Zealand Children's Commissioner: http://www.occ.org.nz/.

Your rights! Your say. Website for Children's Rights Director for England: https://www.rights4me.org/home.cfm.

8

Strengthening practice

Key Points

- In the past decades child protection practice has become increasingly demanding, creating significant challenges both for workers and supervisors. Identifying and extending the knowledge base is increasingly important as workers face the challenges of contemporary practice environments.
- Developing ways of sharpening critical reasoning skills within the context of reflective supervision is one way of strengthening practice within this complex environment.
- Creating meaningful supervision environments and professional development opportunities that address the particular needs of child protection workers is important if services are to protect the interests of children.

Child protection work inevitably involves uncertainty, ambiguity and fallibility. The knowledge base is limited, predictions about the child's future welfare are imperfect, and there is no definitive way of balancing the conflicting rights of parents and children. ... It is hard to imagine circumstances that pose a greater challenge to reasoning skills ... (Munro, 2002: p. 1–2)

These insightful words by Eileen Munro will resonate with anyone who has worked in child protection and has had to make critical decisions about the care and safety of a child. Decisions in child protection can often go one way or the other, and when workers are making them they have no way of knowing whether the rejected alternative might have made more of a difference. Overestimating the risk to a child can result in a child being removed from the care of a family unnecessarily or prematurely, resulting in damage to attachment bonds, alienation from family and potentially an uncertain care future for the child (Connolly and Doolan, 2007). Equally, underestimating risk may result in a child remaining unprotected, whilst indecision and delay leaves everyone in a state of uncertainty and important momentum is lost in terms of securing positive solutions. Supervision provides a critical support for social work decision-making, offering ways in which workers can navigate what can often seem a permeable boundary between safety and harm.

Whilst there have been variations over time in clarifying the functions of supervision, in general most agree that there are at least three main functions in the context of statutory practice: the administrative; the educative; and the supportive functions (Kadushin, 1992). Summarizing the literature, Field (2008) notes that over the years writers have considered systemic approaches that have explored issues of professional dangerousness and organizational challenges (for example, Morrison, 2001; Hughes and Pengelly, 1997); issues of power and control within supervision (for example, Kadushin, 1992; Hawkins and Shohet, 1989) and supervision in the context of anti-discriminatory practice (Brown and Bourne, 1996). Reflecting on the literature of the past thirty years or so it is clear that there has been ongoing attention to supervision, and more recently there have been advancements in the development of supervision within the particular context of child protection and family support practice (for an excellent online resource see Gibbs et al., 2009). However, despite critical reports in the UK which argue strongly for the importance of good supervision to frontline practitioners (Laming, 2003) there are some indications that supervision practice can be patchy and sometimes non-existent (Community Care, 2009). Responding to the particular needs of child protection workers requires specific attention to context and the ways in which it impacts on critical reasoning, professional judgement-making and practice within family and professional systems. In this chapter we will explore an integrated set of ideas that argues for the importance of a nested framework for child protection supervision that includes: a broader knowledge base that supports child and family welfare practice; three additional key elements that we consider to be important to safe practice, and; a systems-focused model of supervision developed as a mechanism for honing critical reasoning and practice judgement skills (figure 8.1).

The knowledge context for child and family welfare supervision practice

In broad terms a systemic conceptual framework provides a strong foundation for understanding child protection and family support practice. In fact, it is difficult to imagine practising with children and

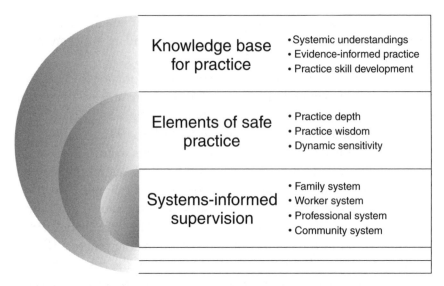

Figure 8.1 A nested model of child protection supervision

families without appreciating the ways in which differing systems influence the dynamics of a child's care and safety. Indeed systemic thinking has had a significant and enduring influence on social work practice and theorizing more generally. Professionals in child welfare are constantly interacting with a range of systems – family systems, professional and organizational systems, and systems across the wider community. And of course, each system will have further systems of significance to its functioning. For example, families extend outwardly to include broader kinship networks. Practitioners work within and across professional boundaries. Each interaction across this complex network of systems has the potential to impact on practice and the way in which practice is undertaken. Differing dynamics within systems can inhibit or support change and a key function of supervision is to help practitioners explore where the potential barriers and solutions lie.

Over time, practice in child protection has changed enormously. In the past decades practice has become increasingly demanding, creating significant challenges both for workers and supervisors. Identifying and extending the knowledge base is increasingly important as workers face the challenges of contemporary practice environments. Beyond the broader systemic analysis it is clear that there are some fundamental knowledge areas that are important to safe practice within statutory systems of child and family welfare. These includes: the evidence base supporting good practice; the practice skills needed to give effect to good practice, and the professional context that is so critical in creating an environment within which good practice can flourish.

In recent years practice frameworks capturing both the evidence base and values supporting good practice have been developed and can provide foundational knowledge for professional practice (see Chapter 3). Typically they include key messages relating to children's development, parental functioning, and the risk factors that impact on children's safety, such as issues of mental health, domestic violence, or patterns of offending. In addition, most countries now have website resources that support child and family welfare practice, for example, *Research in Practice*; *Australian Institute of Family Studies*; and the *Canadian Child Welfare Research Portal*. These provide valuable resources for supervisors offering a means through which professionals can maintain currency with practice developments and research. Given the critical importance of supervision in protective services, creating specific supervision portals within these important websites would serve to both crystallize and extend supervision as a practice in accessible ways for supervisors within the field.

In addition to the evidence base that supports safe practice, there is clearly a skill base that both practitioners and supervisors need to develop if the work is to be done well. Skill development represents a knowledge component that interfaces with the practical expectations of the work and supervisors need to be supported to both engage with this practice knowledge base and to model and coach practice skills. Coaching and modeling is a supervision activity that is informed by learning theory and notions of reflective practice. Supervisors will not necessarily have gained these skills through their own practice experiences, and assumptions are sometimes made that because people are skilled in practice they will necessarily have the competencies that equip them for supervision practice. Whilst this may be true, it is useful to explore a set of practice knowledge and competencies that supervisor will need over and above the practitioner knowledge base. This includes a range of areas. For example, team building knowledge and skills are important in enabling supervisors to harness the strengths and capacity of the people they work with. Familiarity with learning theory assists supervisors in the coaching and modeling of skill development and to present knowledge in the context of diverse learning environments. Building team capability is also set within the context of organizational learning and understandings of organizational change. Child protection operates within a complex professional context, influenced by organizational, cross disciplinary and community interfaces. Supervisors and team leaders have a special role in creating a positive working environment within the context of child protection. This includes stakeholder management and building cross-agency and interdisciplinary relationships and confidence both inside and outside the organization. The potential for supervisors and team leaders to influence the culture of an organization cannot be underestimated. Knowing how organizational systems function and being able to get the most out of stakeholder relationships can be critical to supporting positive change and development within a child protection system. Whilst some people are naturally able in this regard, most will nevertheless benefit from leadership training and the kind of support that helps them to be solution-focused within this most complex area of work. Utilizing organizational theory to inform collaborative practices will help to explore the ways in which collaboration and stakeholder engagement can realistically strengthen contemporary systems of response.

Additional key elements to safe practice

In addition to the broad knowledge context that supports good supervision three key elements supporting safe practice in child protection have been incorporated into our nested conceptual framework: practice depth; practice wisdom; and dynamic sensitivity.

Practice depth

In recent years writers have expressed concern about the ways in which English speaking child protection jurisdictions have been challenged by the increased demands of contemporary practice (Munro, 2011; Ferguson, 2004; Connolly and Doolan, 2007; Lonne et al., 2009). Surges in the notification rates of children perceived to be at risk, high levels of media attention when things go wrong, and a generalized emphasis on managerial solutions have created unintended consequences. Efforts toward greater efficiency have threatened processes of engagement with families as practitioners adopt a one-size-fits-all model that can provide a 'quick fix' so the case can be closed. Ferguson (2004: p. 211) aptly captures this swift movement of families through the child protection system as a 'conveyor-belt' practice. Building on Ferguson's ideas, Chapman and Field (2007) explore levels of practice depth that have the potential to strengthen practice (figure 8.2). They identify two additional levels: pragmatic practice which is characterized by general compliance with policy and guidelines, moderate engagement and efficient throughput of work; and practice that is characterized by critical reflection; interrogation of reasoning; principled decision-making and responsiveness to families.

Because practice operates within a fluid and pressured environment, movement across the practice depth levels are necessary and generally inevitable. Indeed, there will be times when a pragmatic approach is exactly what is needed to meet the needs of a family. What is important, nevertheless, is that we understand the drivers of practice and the ways in which this can impact on a worker's ability to practice in greater depth.

Practice wisdom

Practice wisdom is the repository of knowledge that is gained by experience over time. Trevithick (2007) calls this 'practice knowledge'. Often, practice wisdom is implicit and difficult to clearly articulate. In part intuitive, is it built through repeated practice experience that

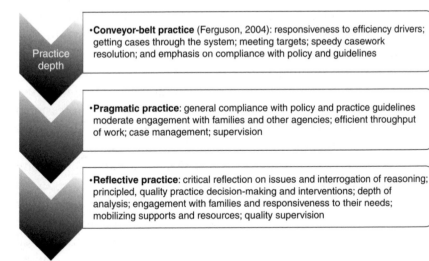

Figure 8.2 Understanding practice depth (adapted from Chapman and Field, 2007)

a worker can call on during practice encounters, and when thinking through complex child protection issues. Practice wisdom is important in the context of supervision not only with respect to what the supervisor brings, but also the ways in which supervision itself can be used as a means of strengthening practice wisdom both for the supervisor and the practitioner.

Creating group supervision opportunities is a good way of building capacity and strengthening both practice knowledge and wisdom across teams of workers. As we noted in Chapter 3, based on Turnell and Edward's (1999) 'Signs of Safety' work, practitioners in the US state of Minnesota established a group supervision consult model to strengthen practice decision-making (Lohrbach, 2008). The nature of the group process means that capability within the team strengthens as workers learn from both the positive and challenging aspects of each other's practice. In essence as well as being capacity-building processes, they also strengthen and build practice wisdom.

Dynamic sensitivity

Dynamic sensitivity is connected to a broader systems analysis, but specifically focuses on the human dynamics that influence the work within child protection and family support practice. It relates to cultural thinking and the dynamics that cause us to interpret our experiences in certain ways (Connolly, 2003). Dynamics of parallel experience, for example, where a worker's experience resonates with that of a service user, has the potential to enhance their helpfulness through greater insight, or it may create blind spots in both thinking and practice. Frightening events or experiences of intimidation in practice can cause workers to react in ways that they may not do otherwise. Or there may be dominating dynamics within the professional or organizational system where professional or agency mandates push practice in ways that do not resonate with the interests of the people receiving the service. Sensitivity to these dynamics within supervision creates opportunity for issues to be considered within the context of a trusted relationship, and in ways that appropriately normalize or challenge experiences and responses in practice. The importance of a supervision relationship that is built on trust is also fundamental to the systems-informed model of supervision that we now explore below.

Systems-informed supervision

The broad knowledge context and the three key elements of safe practice we have discussed so far provide us with a good foundation for exploring systems approaches to supervision. The systems-informed model that we now outline works on the basis that solutions are more likely to be found across a range of system dimensions: the client system; the worker system; the professional system; and the community system. When practitioners get stuck and where solutions seem beyond reach, it is easy to assume that the problem rests with the family – they are resistant to change, or the problems are just too complex. This assumption is based on a one-dimensional approach to problem solving in that solutions are to be found in one location, or one area of the practice system. At one time or another, most practitioners have found themselves going round and round in circles unable to impact on what seem to be intractable family problems. Whilst barriers to progress may indeed rest within the context of the family dynamics, it could just as easily be located in other areas of the practice system. This is where a systemic analysis encourages us to consider a broader set of possibilities, including the influence of the worker, the organization, and community network (figure 8.3). We will now explore each of these quadrants and consider them in the context of what has already been identified as elements of safe practice.

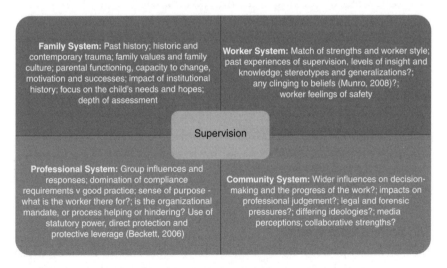

Figure 8.3 A systemic model of child protection supervision

The client system

A family's views about their involvement with protective services is likely to be influenced by a range of factors, such as their experiences of disadvantage, their past experiences of child welfare agencies, and their experience of historic and contemporary trauma. Indeed, talking about a 'family's view' as if it is coherent in its articulation and expression can underestimate what can be competing voices within a family as members agree or disagree on a range of family matters. As Taylor and White (2000: p. 11) note practitioners may experience pressure when confronted by competing versions of the family's story:

> Any work with couples or families may well involve attempts by individuals to recruit the professional into their own particular version of events.

It is a human propensity to bring together information and interpret it according to individual or group beliefs, understandings and priorities. It is also human to try and convince others that our interpretation of the facts is the correct one. Throughout this process dismissal of information or explanations that do not fit with preferred interpretations of events is not uncommon. Dynamic sensitivity helps workers think about how they might explore family life stories, values and thinking in ways that help to identify what has sustained the problems over time, and open up creative and different ways of seeking solutions (Watzlawick et al., 1974). This requires a depth of assessment and intervention that is beyond what Ferguson (2004) identifies as 'conveyor belt' practice, requiring also a depth of knowledge about family and parental functioning, children's development, and the ways in which abuse and neglect intersect with these.

KEY PRACTICE QUESTIONS 8.1

1. In what practical ways might a supervisor help a worker to avoid being captured by dominant views within a family?
2. How might subject knowledge help to better understand the client system?

The professional system

Berlin (2002: p. 269) argues that we have a 'mixture of motives' when practising social work. Professional practice requires that we engage, whilst also maintaining a degree of distance, or at least stepping back, so we can work in the best interests of children. In this way, 'it requires us to balance openness, spontaneity, and involvement with professional discipline' (ibid). This is a paradox that can create issues and conflicts in practice. Professional/client relationships are different from our ordinary day-to-day interactions we have with friends and colleagues. Professional relationships require a high level of personal insight and knowledge. Parallel worker/client experiences can give a worker greater insight into the complexity of the work, or it can create feelings that interfere with a worker's ability to confront issues or to see things clearly with a reasonable degree of objectivity. Shulman (1993: p. 190) has noted that 'analysis of worker practice often reveals moments when workers felt like confronting a client but did not because of their own discomfort'. Shutting down difficult conversations that may have been helpful in exploring issues of safety and harm is an example of this.

In child protection, professionals are exposed to experiences that many people would find abhorrent, distressing and often frightening. These experiences can cause a worker to disengage from the intensity of the work. Feelings of being physically unsafe or having been exposed to intimidation or violence can result in professionals working remotely, for example, resorting to the use of telephones rather than direct client contact. Or the worker may avoid the family all together. And yet professional exposure to violence in child protection work can sometimes be 'the elephant in the room' during supervision. Workers may not want to talk about their experiences seeing it as a failure on their part. Or they may talk about it only to experience the conversation being shut down when others make light of it, or perhaps feel equally powerless to do anything about it.

KEY PRACTICE QUESTIONS 8.2

1. How can supervision avoid turning into a therapy session when exploring the worker system?
2. How can supervisors ensure that their supervision conversations remain purposeful and professional when exploring the worker system?

The organizational system

Organizational systems and mandates inevitably impact on the way in which practice is undertaken within agencies. Beddoe and Maidment

(2009: p. 26) note the impact that managerial approaches can have on the ability of workers to advocate on behalf of clients:

> Managerialist language associated with achieving key performance indicators, managing risk and avoiding legal liability tends now to overshadow principal social work concerns relating to addressing client oppression and poverty.…

In the context of child protection and family support practice, such advocacy includes collaborative problem solving with families, providing contexts within which families can work toward positive solutions, and managing the tension between child protection and family support. Adopting family engagement strategies within child protection requires the support of the organizational system. Messages from senior managers can powerfully influence practice. For example, reinforcement of a one-size-fits all approach that focuses on targets and efficiency measures can interfere with a worker's ability to engage with families, and to get the most out of family engagement strategies. Supervisors may find themselves the meat in the sandwich – on the one hand they are required to ensure that the service is efficient in terms of its resources, on the other hand they may see that supporting a more engaging response with families is better in the longer-term as it has the potential to avoid re-referrals into the system. Exploring what may be undue domination of compliance requirements over good practice responses in supervision will help to distinguish between actual and perceived tension between organizational mandate and professional practice. When a practice system has been pushed into an 'assess and close the case as soon as possible' mode, it can become the prevailing culture of practice over time. In these situations, even when alternative messages attempt to strengthen practice depth, the prevailing practice culture can continue to dominate. Creating opportunities for dialogue exploring the ways in which the organization helps or hinders practice facilitates the possibility of doing some things differently. Supervisors can be critically important to the creation of a positive practice culture within an organization. If the supervisor is constrained by the tension, then supervision will struggle to provide a solution context.

Organizational systems also mandate professional power and it is important that both practitioners and supervisors consider the ways in which power dynamics can influence practice. Beckett (2006: p. 157) explores two ways in which statutory powers may be used: explicitly through *direct protection*, where a social worker takes action to protect, or through a process of *protective leverage*. Protective leverage uses statutory power implicitly to encourage compliance. Here the worker does not take direct protective action but the client knows they could do so in the event of non-compliance. In many respects explicit coercive power is more straightforward and transparent and when legal steps are taken a formal process provides accountability checks and balances for actions that are taken. Protective leverage, however, does not have the same checks and balances, often becoming part of a general social work approach within a statutory practice setting. This is something that Beckett (2006: p. 157) expresses concern about when protective leverage is used broadly and even unconsciously:

> I think that we are inclined to greatly underestimate the extent of our implicit powers. Social workers sometimes exercise implicit coercive powers without even realising it, imagining that they are working in a voluntary partnership with service users when in fact service users are complying with their wishes out of fear of the consequences of not doing so.

Understanding the nature of expert power is important therefore to the broader appreciation of the professional system and its impact.

KEY PRACTICE QUESTIONS 8.3

1. How can the organizational system influence practice depth and the development of professional judgement?
2. How might a supervisor promote a positive practice culture when exploring the organizational system quadrant?

The community system

The dominance of cultural thinking can extend beyond the boundaries of the worker/client, and the organizational system. Professionals involved may differ in their opinions about the ways in which a child protection investigation or intervention should or could be managed. When exploring the community system quadrant, it is helpful to identify the drivers of practice across the professional sphere. This will also identify whether they are helping or hindering the work. For example, in the context of professional discourses, writers have noted the dominance of legal approaches in the context of child protection enquiries (Sheehan, 2009; Braye and Preston-Shoot, 2002). Supervision provides an opportunity to discuss law and how it can influence practice either directly or indirectly. Sheehan (2009: p. 342) encourages us to:

> ...know and understand the ways in which the law can be used as an important tool to support human rights and client self-determination... and the ways in which interpretations of the law can disadvantage clients and work against their right to agency and self-determination.

Most countries are now signatories to UNCROC and as a consequence child protection systems are charged with responsibilities to uphold its principles. National and state child welfare legislation is generally influenced by UNCROC, and it is important that practice systems create time to consider practice in the context of both UNCROC and the general principles underpinning child protection law.

Other potentially dominating discourses emerge across multidisciplinary contexts, for example, the 'damage model' articulated by Wolin and Wolin (1993: p. 13):

> Troubled families are seen as toxic agents, like bacteria or viruses, and the survivors are regarded as victims of their parents' poisonous secretions. Children, according to the Damage Model, are vulnerable, helpless, and locked into the family. The best survivors can do is to cope or contain the family's harmful influence at considerable cost to themselves.

Although somewhat provocative in its language, this quote does illustrate the power of deficit discourses and the ways in which these ideas can define and lead intervention efforts (Healy, 2005).

Within the community system, professionals may also be influenced by dominant attitudes across communities, including their own local environment. People across local neighbourhoods may hold strong views about issues, and may generalize or promote stereotypical attitudes. These, along with the expression of other dominant ideologies, can be influential over time and can find their way into professional thinking creating the potential for more punitive or conservative approaches. Similarly writers have noted that media influences can be strong in creating more risk averse responses in child protection (Connolly and Doolan, 2007; Mansell, 2006). Exploring these issues in supervision can help to identify if such views are interfering with the ability to find practice solutions.

1. How might high profile media criticism relating to child protection impact on practice?
2. How might good practice be enhanced by strong legal schemes?
3. What other professional ideologies might impact positively or negatively on practice?

Strengthening practice in child protection

Strengthening supervision models to address particular issues relating to child protection and family welfare practice has the potential to nurture creativity, enhance professional judgement-making, and create learning environments for both practitioners and supervisors. Questioning practice and challenging in the context of a supportive relationship can also help to identify support needs and the kind of training and development needed to further build skill and expertise. As we draw toward the end of this book it is clear to us that there are some fundamental knowledge areas that are important to safe practice within statutory systems of child and family welfare. Summarized these include: the knowledge and evidence base; practice skills; analytical strengths; and professional context (figure 8.4).

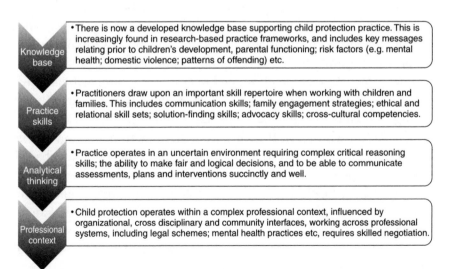

Figure 8.4 Knowledge areas important for safe practice in child protection

In earlier chapters we talked about the importance of developing strong practice frameworks that are based on evidence and a good understanding of what works. These provide critical foundational knowledge for professional practice in child protection. It is a knowledge base that practitioners need to have at their fingertips, familiar enough to be drawn upon in their day-to-day practice. Building further upon this, more complex understandings of parenting in the context of vulnerability – mental illness, disability, and addiction is also important. The dynamics of family violence, and patterns of offending behaviour can be critical when working with families, particularly in the context of intergenerational abuse. Practitioners need to be able to both articulate the professional knowledge base, and demonstrate its integration in practice.

Clearly practice skills are also very important when working in child protection. Managing the dynamic practice tension between child protection and family support, and persevering with engagement in the context of resistance is not easy. Traditionally supervisors provide feedback on a practitioner's self-report of their activities within the field. As an alternative to responding to what they are told happens in field practice, we would argue the value of supervisors observing practice from time to time, and providing feedback on the actual process of worker/client engagement. This type of action/reflection dynamic within supervision, that includes observed practice and feedback, helps to ensure that practice remains purposeful over time and prevents against the work becoming automated or stagnant.

Supervisors and team leaders need to sharpen their analytical skills so they can support workers in the context of complex practice decision-making. This includes helping workers to communicate clearly both verbally and in writing. In the same way that practitioners hone their skills through direct observation within the context of action/feedback/ reflection, supervision skills can also be honed through observed practice and feedback that focuses particularly on areas of analytical decision and judgement-making. In this way group and individual supervision sessions can become laboratories of learning where practitioners and supervisors take part in a process of collaborative learning and reflective practice. Occasionally recording supervision sessions using video technology, if it is available, is also a good way of noting skill development over time providing opportunity for self-critique and feedback from peers.

Importantly, child protection practice works constantly at the interface of interdisciplinary work. As we have noted earlier, this community interface can influence the work significantly and practitioners need to know how to handle themselves in multidisciplinary settings. Keeping abreast of the knowledge base provides greater professional confidence and the ability to withstand the professional influences that impact negatively on the child's safe care. In this sense it is important to understand the ways in which professional dynamics support or hinder practice. Strengthening professional practice, being able to clearly articulate practice decisions, demonstrate critical reasoning in decision-making and present well in legal, medical or other disciplinary environments builds both confidence and respect when working across professional boundaries.

Practitioners who demonstrate strengths in practice often move into positions of responsibility as team leaders or supervisors. Assumptions are frequently made that because people are skilled in practice they will necessarily be good supervisors. Whilst this may well be true, there is nevertheless a body of knowledge and sets of practice skills that supervisor's need over and above the practitioner's knowledge base. A supervision knowledge base for practice includes familiarity with learning theory and aspects of organizational management including practical ideas about how to build responsive teams. Supervisors need feedback on their supervision skills; their ability to harness the strengths and capacity of teams; and to present knowledge in the context of diverse learning environments. Supervisors also need to be experts in analytical thinking and to be able to work with practitioners to both strengthen critical reasoning and ensure that communications are well justified and succinct.

Writers have noted the importance of leadership across the professional system (Gibbs et al., 2009). Supervisors and team leaders have a special role in creating a positive working environment for workers in child protection. This includes stakeholder management and building cross-agency and interdisciplinary relationships and building confidence both inside and outside the organization. The potential for supervisors and team leaders to influence the culture of an organization cannot be underestimated. When leaders are positive and collaborative across the professional system, there is a greater chance of staff also being positive about the work. Knowing how organizational systems function and being able to get the most out of stakeholder relationships can help to support positive change and development within a child protection system. Whilst some people are naturally able in this regard, most people will benefit from leadership training and the kind of support that helps them to be solution-focused within this most complex area of work.

Strengthening practice – an organizational imperative

Having argued the importance of worker and supervisor skills in strengthening practice at the frontline, the ways in which organizations provide quality practice-supportive conditions is also essential. In her review of child protection in England, Munro (2010: p. 8) noted:

> Compliance with regulation and rules often drives professional practice more than sound judgement drawn from the professional relationship and interaction with a child, young person and family.

The review concluded that a highly prescriptive organizational culture has the potential to undermine the development of knowledge and skill in child protection practice (Munro, 2011), and recommends the creation of a better balance between prescription and the enhancement of professional judgement and expertise. Creating a succinct, unambiguous set of expectations is a challenge when child protection policies are written urgently and defensively (Connolly and Smith, 2010). Systems have nevertheless taken up the challenge of rewriting prescriptive and lengthy policies. For example, in New Zealand operational policies have been reduced to a limited set of 'must-dos' (see www.practicecentre.cyf. govt.nz). Beyond these 'must-dos' discussion documents explore ways in which these must-dos can be done well:

> Rather than focus on procedures to drive practice, discussion documents encourage a greater emphasis on the exercising of professional judgement and good professional decision-making. (Connolly and Smith, 2010: p. 25)

The Munro review identifies a number of ways in which organizations can support effective practice in child protection. Importantly Munro argues for a more varied career path for practitioners to both strengthen the frontline and maintain experienced and skilled workers within the frontline workforce:

> The current career structure should be replaced with one that allows more opportunity for people to stay in practice while gaining seniority within the organization. ... the development of individual expertise and of the

profession's knowledge base has been seriously hampered by a career pattern requiring people to leave practice in order to get promoted. ... each local authority should have a designated Principal Child and Family Social Worker who is still actively involved in practice and who would help the development of practice expertise in that authority. (Munro, 2011: p. 133)

Creating a stronger voice for social work in England through the establishment of a Chief Social Worker as an advisor to government is an indication of the importance the review places on professional practice and the building of professional knowledge and expertise. Newly formed Colleges of Social Work in England and Australia will also play an important part in providing leadership and promoting quality practice and expertise. These developments augur well for the strengthening of practice in child and family welfare practice.

Conclusion

Supporting people who work in child protection is critical to the development of a stable workforce. There is no question that the work has become more complex over time, and that workers often find themselves challenged by difficult dynamics across client, professional and community systems. Child protection work can, nevertheless, be extremely rewarding and even in the most difficult work environment it is possible to create professional strength and resilience. Purposeful supervision can play an important part in supporting staff and building strong practice systems, and investment in supervision support and professional development for staff is likely to see positive outcomes both with respect to worker satisfaction and improved service delivery. More broadly, agencies that meet the challenges of contemporary practice and demanding organizational contexts have the potential to build stronger and more effective services for children at risk.

FURTHER READING

Gibbs, J., Dwyer, J. and Vivekananda, K. (2009) *Leading Practice: A Resource Guide for Child Protection Frontline and Middle Managers*, available online from: http://www.cyf.vic.gov.au/__data/assets/pdf_file/0008/414494/leading-practice-resource-guide.pdf.

Social Work Now, volume 40, August 2008, special edition dedicated to supervision. Available online from http://www.cyf.govt.nz/documents/about-us/publications/social-work-now/social-work-now-40-aug08.pdf.

USEFUL WEBSITES

The Canadian *Centres for Excellence for Children's Wellbeing* provides an excellent child welfare research portal that also offers free subscription to a monthly research watch. Available online from http://www.cwrp.ca/?utm_source=CECW-CEPB+E-Newsletter&utm_campaign=aa93c53a10-RW_English_January_14_2010&utm_medium=email.

Iriss is a Scottish website that provides a rich resource for workers within the social services. Available online from http://www.iriss.org.uk/.

The UK website *Research in Practice* provides research and policy updates, and a range of information based resources for practitioners. Available online from http://www.rip.org.uk/.

Concluding thoughts

In this book we have looked at the ways in which child protection work can be enhanced by a strong knowledge base, innovative professional practices, and supportive organizational contexts. Creating strong services for children is not an easy task and in recent times most English speaking child protection systems have undergone reform and development, often in response to challenging reviews that have exposed weaknesses in statutory service responses. Systems will continue to evolve and change, but it is significant that many recent reforms have emphasized systemic issues and called for integrated responses that support in depth, quality practice.

As we have considered the issues we hope we have illustrated the complexities in providing effective services for children, and the importance of services being child-centred. In many ways child protection work has become very adult-centred as professionals give primacy to the words, views and interpretations of adults. Yet children can provide crucial information about their experiences. Listening to the voices of children and engaging with their concerns will not only help us to understand their particular needs, but will also help to create a context of advocacy where children's rights can be advanced.

Whilst being advocates for children, effective child protection practice also requires that we remain family-focused and that we engage with families in ways that will support child safety and care. As we noted in Chapter 2, child protection workers manage fundamental tensions in supporting families whilst negotiating pathways through complex child protection matters. This tension rests at the heart of child protection practice and tests the expertise of even the most experienced of practitioners. Working transparently and confronting issues within a supportive practice context is, nevertheless, possible in child protection work and working collaboratively with families is more likely to facilitate good outcomes for children. Engaging with extended families and harnessing the resources of kinship networks also has the potential to increase the safety support system surrounding children at risk.

Finally, supporting the work of child protection requires that we pay attention to the needs of professionals working daily with the most vulnerable of our children. As we noted in our final chapter, child protection is a most complex area of work, and one that challenges both decision-making and professional judgement. When something goes wrong and a tragedy occurs it not only touches the very hearts of communities, it also critically impacts on the professionals involved in the child's care. Ignited often by aggressive media reporting, it is not surprising when grieving communities then demand answers and seek assurances that it will never happen again. The culture of blame that has nevertheless emerged in recent years, whilst satisfying the need for a scapegoat, does little to support the majority of workers who strive to provide strong services for children. Rather it propels systems to seek quick fixes through the introduction of more rules and tools – naïve responses that has the effect of disabling systems and ultimately creating greater risk for children.

Building the sector strategically creates opportunities for a more coherent approach to strengthening child protection responses. In the end, building effective services involves the development of a complex mix of purposeful responses to children and families. Systems that recognize this complexity will avoid the pressure to respond with quick fixes that fail to endure over time. Rather, they will adopt a more coherent approach that prioritizes services delivered by universal, targeted and specialist systems, providing responses based on need. Investing in this broader service agenda has the potential to better meet the needs of children and families, and to provide more rewarding working environments that encourage the retention of experienced and skilled workers.

References

Ainsworth, F. (1997) 'Foster Care Research in US and Australia: An Update', *Children Australia*, 22(2), pp. 9–16.

Alderson, P. (2001) 'Research by Children', *International Journal of Social Research Methodology*, 4(2), pp. 139–153.

Alderson, P. and Morrow, V. (2004) *Ethics, Social Research and Consulting with Children and Young People*, Ilford: Barnardo's.

Aldgate, J. and Bradley, M. (1999) *Supporting Families Through Short-term Fostering*, London: The Stationary Office.

Aldgate, J. and McIntosh, M. (2006) *Looking After the Family: A Study of Children Looked After in Kinship Care in Scotland, Edinburgh*, Edinburgh: Social Work Inspection Agency, available from www.scotland.gov.uk/Resource/Doc/129074/0030729.pdf, retrieved 14 March 2010.

Allard, A. S. (2002) *A Case Study Investigation into the Implementation of the Children (Leaving Care) Act 2000*, London: NCH.

Allen Consulting Group (2008) *Inverting the Pyramid: Enhancing Systems for Protecting Children*. Commissioned by Australian Research Alliance for Children and Youth. Available online from http://www.aracy.org.au/cmsdocuments/REP_Inverting_the_Pyramid_Enhancing_Systems_for_Protecting_Children_2009.pdf.

Allen, J. and Vostanis, P. (2005) 'The Impact of Abuse and Trauma on a Developing Child: An Evaluation of a Training Programme for Foster Carers and Supervising Social Workers', *Adoption and Fostering*, 29(3), pp. 68–81.

Allen, M. (2003) *Factors that Influence Young People Leaving Care*, York: Joseph Rowntree Foundation.

Anderson, G. R. (2005) 'Family Group Conferencing and Child Welfare: Contributions and Challenges', in J. Pennell and G. Anderson, *Widening the Circle: The Practice and Evaluation of Family Group Conferencing with Children, Youths and Their Families*, Washington DC: NASW Press, pp. 221–236.

Appel, A. E. and Holden, G. W. (1998) 'The Co-occurrence of Spouse and Physical Child Abuse: A Review and Appraisal', *Journal of Family Psychology*, 12, pp. 578–599.

Argent, H. (2006) *Top Ten Tips for Placing Children in Permanent Families*, London: British Association for Adopting and Fostering.

Arney, F. and Scott, D. (2010) *Working with Vulnerable Families: A Partnership Approach*, New York: Cambridge University Press.

Ashley, C. and Nixon, P. (2007) *Family Group Conferences: Where Next? Policies and Practices for the Future*, London: Family Rights Group.

Association of the Directors of Children's Services (ADCS) (2010) *Child Protection Activities in Councils on the Rise,* ADCS http://www.adcs.org.uk/ retrieved June 2010.

Atwool, N. (1997) 'Making Connections: Attachment and Resilience', in N. J. Taylor and A. B. Smith (eds), *Enhancing Children's Potential: Minimising Risk and Maximising Resilience,* Proceedings of the Children's Issues Centre, Second Child and Family Policy Conference, 2–4 July 1997, Dunedin.

Atwool, N. (2005) 'Working with Adults Who Are Parenting', in M. Nash, R. Munford and K. O'Donoghue (eds), *Social Work Theories in Action,* London: Jessica Kingsley Publishers.

Atwool, N. (2007) 'The Role of Secure Attachment as a Protective Factor for Vulnerable Infants,' *Social Work Now,* 38, December, pp. 11–20.

Australian Children's Commissioners and Children's Guardians (2009) *How Australian Kids See The World: Commemorating 20 Years of the UN Convention on the Rights of the Child,* Sydney: New South Wales Government.

Australian Institute of Family Studies (2009) *Child Abuse and Neglect Statistics,* Resource Sheet No 1, available from: http://www.aifs.gov.au/nch/pubs/sheets/rs1/rs1.html, retrieved 23 January 2010.

Australian Institute of Health and Welfare (2009) *Child Protection Australia 2007–08* (Child Welfare Series No. 45). Canberra: AIHW.

Australian Institute of Health and Welfare (2010) *Adoptions Australia 2008–09* (Child Welfare Series No. 48). Cat. No. CWS 36. Canberra: AIHW.

Axford, N. and Little, M. (2006) 'Refocusing Children's Services Towards Prevention: Lessons from the Literature', *Children and Society,* 20(4), pp. 299–312.

Bacon, H. and Richardson, S. (2001) 'Attachment Theory and Child Abuse: An Overview of the Literature for Practitioners', *Child Abuse Review,* 10(6), pp. 377–397.

Baker, M. (2001) *Families, Labour and Love,* Crows Nest: Allen and Unwin.

Ball, D. and Wilson, M. (2002) 'The Prevalence and Persistence of Low Income Among New Zealand Children: Indicative Measures from Benefit Dynamics Data', [Electronic version] *Social Policy Journal of New Zealand,* 18, pp. 92–117.

Ban, P. (1994) 'Preliminary Findings on Family Decision Making Project in the Victorian Child Protection System', *Australian Social Work,* 47(1), pp. 34–36.

Ban, P. (1996) 'Implementing and Evaluating Family Group Conferences with Children and Families in Victoria Australia', in J. Hudson, A. Morris, G. Maxwell and B. Galaway (eds), *Family Group Conferences: Perspectives on Policy and Practice,* Australia: Federation.

Bannon, M. J. and Carter, Y. H (eds) (2003) *Protecting Children from Abuse and Neglect in Primary Care,* Oxford: Oxford University Press.

Barn, R., Andrew, L. and Mantovani, N. (2005) *Life After Care: The Experiences of Young People from Different Ethnic Groups,* York: Joseph Rowntree Foundation.

Barter, K. (2001) 'Building Community: A Conceptual Framework for Child Protection', *Child Abuse Review,* 10(4), pp. 262–278.

Bath, H. (2009) 'The Changing Role of Residential Care in Australia', *Social Work Now,* 43, August, pp. 21–31.

Beckett, C. (2006) *Essential Theory for Social Work Practice*, London: Sage Publications.

Beddoe, E. and Maidment, J. (2009) *Mapping Knowledge for Social Work Practice: Critical Intersections*, South Melbourne: Cengage Learning.

Beek, M. and Schofield, G. (2004) *Providing a Secure Long Term Base in Foster Care*, London: BAAF.

Benevolent Society (2009) *Supporting Kinship Care: Towards a New Practice Framework*, available from http://www.bensoc.org.au/uploads/documents/ SupportingKinshipCareSnapshot.pdf, retrieved 7 July 2010.

Berger, L. M. (2005) 'Income, Family Characteristics, and Physical Violence Toward Children', *Child Abuse and Neglect*, 29, pp. 107–133.

Berlin, S. B. (2002) *Clinical Social Work Practice: A Cognitive-intergrative Perspective*, New York: Oxford University Press.

Berrick, J. D., Frasch, K. and Fox, A. (2000) 'Note on Research Methodology. Assessing Children's Experiences of Out-of-home Care: Methodological Challenges and Opportunities', *Social Work Research*, 24(2), pp. 119–127.

Berridge, D. (1997) *Foster Care: A Research Review*, London: HMSO.

Berridge, D. (2005) 'Fostering Now: Messages from Research, A Summary', *Adoption and Fostering*, 29(3), pp. 6–8.

Berzin, S. C. (2006) 'Using Sibling Data to Understand the Impact of Family Group Decision-making on Child Welfare Outcomes', *Children and Youth Services Review*, 28, pp. 1449–1458.

Biehal, N. (2008) *Research on Children In and On The Edge of Care: Where Have We Been and Where Are We Going?* Working Paper no 2345, University of York.

Biehal, N., Ellison, S., Baker, C. and Sinclair, I. (2009) *Characteristics, Outcomes and Meanings of the Three Types of Permanent Placement – Adoption by Strangers, Adoption by Carers and Long Term Foster Care*, London: DCSF.

Billing, A., Ehrle, J. and Kortenkamp, K. (2002) 'Children Cared For By Relatives: What Do We Know About Their Well-being?' *Assessing the New Federalism, Series B, No B-46*, Washington DC: The Urban Institute.

Birchall, E. and Hallett, C. (1995) *Working Together in Child Protection*, London: HMSO.

Birmingham, J., Berry, M. and Bussey, M. (1996) 'Certification for Child Welfare Protective Services Staff Members: The Texas Initiative', [Electronic version] *Child Welfare*, 75(6), pp. 727–740.

Blum, J. and Gray, S. (1987) Strategies for Communicating with Young Children. Seminar presented at the 16th National Symposium on Child Abuse and Neglect, Keystone, CO.

Blumenthal, K. (1983) 'Making Foster Family Care Responsive', in B. McGowan and W. Meezan (eds), *Child Welfare: Current Dilemmas – Future Directions*, Itasca, IL: Peacock.

Braithwaite, V., Harris, N. and Ivec, M. (2009) 'Seeking to Clarify Child Protection's Regulatory Principles', *Communities, Children and Families Australia*, 4(1), pp. 5–21.

Braye, S. and Preston-Shoot, M. (2002) 'Social Work and the Law', in R. Adams, L. Dominelli and M. Payne (eds), *Social Work: Themes, Issues and Critical Debates*, 2nd ed, Basingstoke: Palgrave, pp. 62–73, Ch. 6.

Briar-Lawson, K., Schmid, D. and Harris, N. (1997) 'The Partnership Journey: First Decade', [Electronic version] *Child Welfare*, 55(2), pp. 33–41.

Broad, B. (2001) 'Kinship Care: Supporting Children in Placements with Extended Family and Friends', *Adoption and Fostering*, 25(2), pp. 33–41.

Broad, B. (2004) 'Kinship Care for Children in the UK: Messages from Research, Lessons for Policy and Practice', *European Journal of Social Work*, 7(2), pp. 211–227.

Brodie, I. (2009) *Improving Educational Outcomes for Looked After Children and Young People*, London: C4EO, available from http://www.c4eo.org.uk/themes/vulnerablechildren/default.aspx?themeid=3&accesstypeid=1, retrieved May 2010.

Bromfield, L., Higgins, D., Osborn, A., Panozzo, S. and Richardson, N. (2005) *Out of Home Care in Australia: Messages from the Research*, Australian Institute of Family Studies, Melbourne, available from http://www.aifs.gov.au/nch/pubs/reports/outofhome/outofhome.pdf, retrieved 25 June 2010.

Brown, A. and Bourne, I. (1996) *The Social Work Supervisor*, Buckingham: Open University Press.

Brown, L. (2003) 'Mainstream or Margin? The Current Use of Family Group Conferences in Child Welfare Practice in the UK', *Child and Family Social Work*, 8(4), pp. 331–340.

Brown, L. (2007) 'The Adoption and Implementation of a Service Innovation in a Social Work Setting – A Case Study of Family Group Conferencing in the UK', *Social Policy and Society*, 6(3), pp. 321–332.

Brucker, M., Easterbrook-Smith, S. and Martin, S. (2003) 'Rethinking Residential Services: Issues and Trends', *Social Work Now*, 25, pp. 44–45.

Brudenell, M. and Savage, A. (2000) 'Ordinary People Doing Something Special', *Social Work Now*, 16, pp. 6–12.

Buckley, H. (2000) 'Beyond the Rhetoric: A "Working" Version of Child Protection Practice', [Electronic version] *European Journal of Social Work*, 3(1), pp. 13–24.

Bullock, R., Little, M. and Milham, S. (1993) *Going Home: The Return of Children Separated from Their Families*, Aldershot: Dartmouth.

Burford, G., Connolly, M., Morris, K. and Pennell, J. (2009) *Family Group Decision Making: Annotated Bibliography on Engaging the Family Group in Child Welfare Decision Making*, American Humane Association.

Cairns. K. (2002a) 'Making Sense: The Use of Theory and Research to Support Foster Care', *Adoption and Fostering*, 26(2), pp. 6–13.

Cairns, K. (2002b) *Attachment, Trauma and Resilience: Therapeutic Caring for Children*, London: BAAF.

Calder, M. C. and Horwath, J. (2000) 'Challenging Passive Partnerships with Parents and Children in the Core Group Forum: A Framework for a Proactive Approach', *Child and Family Social Work*, 5, pp. 267–277.

Cameron, G. and Vanderwoerd, J. (1997) *Protecting Children and Supporting Families: Promising Programs and Organizational Realities,* New York: Aldine de Gruyter.

Cameron, M. (2006) *Alternate Dispute Resolution: Aboriginal Models and Practices: Literature Review,* Vancouver, British Columbia, Canada: Ministry of Children and Family Development.

Cashmore, J. and Ainsworth, F. (2003) 'Out-of-home Care: Building a National Research Agenda', *Children Australia,* 28(2), pp. 5–13.

Cashmore, J. and O'Brien, A. (2001) 'Facilitating Participation of Children and Young People in Care', *Children Australia,* 26(4), pp. 10–15.

Chan, J. S., Elliott, J. M., Chow, Y. and Thomas, J. I. (2002) 'Does Professional and Public Opinion in Child Abuse Differ? An Issue of Cross-cultural Policy Implementation', *Child Abuse Review,* 11(6), pp. 359–379.

Chapman, M. and Field, J. (2007) 'Strengthening Our Engagement with Families and Understanding Practice Depth', *Social Work Now,* 38, December, pp. 21–28.

Child Welfare Information Gateway (2008) *Differential Response to Reports of Child Abuse and Neglect,* Issue brief, February. Available from http://www.childwelfare. gov/pubs/issue_briefs/differential_response/differential_response.pdf, retrieved 14 January 2010.

Child, Youth and Family (2007) *Leading for Outcomes.* Available from http://www. cyf.govt.nz/documents/about-us/publications/leading-for-outcomes-year1.pdf, retrieved 30 June 2011.

Child, Youth and Family (2010a) *Areas to Explore When Assessing Family/Whanau Caregivers,* Practice Centre. Available from http://practicecentre.cyf.govt.nz/ policy/caregiver-assessment-and-approval/whanau-caregivers/key-information/ assessing-family-whanau-caregivers.html, retrieved 8 July 2010.

Child, Youth and Family (2010b) *Pathway for Family/Whanau Assessment and Approval,* Child, Youth and Family Practice Centre, available from http://practicecentre.cyf.govt.nz/policy/caregiver-assessment-and-approval/ resources/pathway-for-family-whanau-caregiver-assessment-and-approval.html, retrieved 8 July 2010.

Child, Youth and Family (2011) *The Three Houses Tool,* retrieved from http:// preacticecentre.govt.nz/policy/practice-tools/resources/three-houses-tool.html.

Chipman, R., Wells, S. W. and Johnson, M. A. (2002) 'The Meaning of Quality in Kinship Foster Care: Caregiver, Child, and Worker Perspectives', *Families in Society,* 83(516), pp. 508–521.

Christensen, Pia, and James, Allison (2008) *Research with Children: Perspectives and Practices,* 2nd ed, London: Jessica Kingsley Publishers.

Christie, A. and Mittler, H. (1999) 'Partnership and Core Groups in the Risk Society', *Child and Family Social Work,* 4, pp. 231–240.

Clare, M. (1997) 'The UK "Looking After Children" Project: Fit for Out-of-Home Care Practice in Australia?' *Children Australia,* 22(1), pp. 29–35.

Cleaver, H. (2000) *Fostering Family Contact: A Study of Children, Parents and Foster Carers,* London: The Stationary Office.

Cleaver, H. and Walker, S. (2004) *Assessing Children's Needs and Circumstances: The Impact of the Assessment Framework*, London: Jessica Kingsley Publishers.

Coad, J. and Lewis, A. (2004) *Engaging Children and Young People in Research: A Literature Review for the National Evaluation of the Children's Fund*, London: DCSF.

Colton, M. and Williams, M. (eds) (2006) *Global Perspectives in Foster Family Care*, Lyme Regis: Russell House.

Commonwealth of Australia (2009a) *Protecting Australia's Children is Everyone's Business, National Framework for Protecting Australia's Children, 2009–2020*, available from: http://www.coag.gov.au/coag_meeting_outcomes/2009–04-30/docs/child_protection_framework.pdf, retrieved 28 May 2009.

Commonwealth of Australia (2009b) *Protecting Australia's Children is Everyone's Business, National Framework for Protecting Australia's Children: Implementing the First Three-year Action Plan, 2009–2012*, Canberra: ACT.

Community Care (2009) *Unison: High Vacancies and Rising Caseloads Risk Another Baby P*, 26 January 2009, available from: http://www.communitycare.co.uk/Articles/2009/01/26/110535/unison-high-vacancies-and-rising-caseloads-risk-another-baby-p.htm, retrieved 25 January 2010.

Connolly, M. (1999) *Effective Participatory Practice: Family Group Conferencing in Child Protection*, New York: Aldine de Gruyter.

Connolly, M. (2003) 'A Kinship Care Literature Review', *Social Work Now*, 25, pp. 41–43.

Connolly, M. (2004) 'A Perspective on the Origins of Family Group Conferencing', *American Humane Society Issues in Brief*, 1–3, available from http://www.americanhumane.org.

Connolly, M. (2006a) 'Fifteen Years of Family Group Conferencing: Coordinators Talk About Their Experiences in Aotearoa New Zealand', *British Journal of Social Work*, 36(4), pp. 523–540.

Connolly, M. (2006b) 'Upfront and Personal: Confronting Dynamics in the Family Group Conference', *Family Process*, 45(3), September, pp. 345–357.

Connolly, M. (2007) 'Practice Frameworks: Conceptual Maps to Guide Interventions in Child Welfare', *British Journal of Social Work*, 37(5), pp. 825–837.

Connolly, M. (2009) 'Professional Responses: Who Does What in Domestic Violence and Child Protection', *Communities, Children and Families Australia*, 4(1), pp. 34–37.

Connolly, M. and Cashmore, J. (2009) 'Child Welfare Practice', in M. Connolly and L. Harms (eds), *Social Work: Contexts and Practice*, 2nd ed, Melbourne: Oxford University Press, pp. 275–290, Ch. 20.

Connolly, M., Crichton-Hill, Y. and Ward, T. (2006) *Culture and Child Protection: Reflexive Responses*, London: Jessica Kingsley Publishers.

Connolly, M. and Doolan, M. (2007) *Lives Cut Short: Child Death by Maltreatment*, Wellington: Dunmore Press.

Connolly, M. and Healy, K. (2009) Social Work Practice Theories and Frameworks, in M. Connolly and L. Harms, *Social Work: Contexts and Practice*, Melbourne: Oxford University Press, pp. 19–36, Ch. 2.

Connolly, M. and Smith, R. (2010) 'Reforming Child Welfare: An Integrated Approach', *Child Welfare,* 89(3), pp. 9–31.

Connolly, M. and Ward, T. (2008) *Morals Rights and Practice in the Human Services: Effective and Fair Decision-making in Health, Social Care and Criminal Justice,* London: Jessica Kingsley Publishers.

Conway, E. E., Jr. (1998) 'Nonaccidental Head Injury in Infants: "The Shaken Baby Syndrome Revisited"' [Electronic version] *Pediatric Annals,* 27(10), pp. 677–690.

Corby, B. (1993) *Child Abuse: Towards a Knowledge Base,* Buckingham: Open University Press.

Council of Australian Governments (2009) *Protecting Australia's Children is Everyone's Business, National Framework for Protecting Australia's Children, 2009–2020.* Available from www.coag.gov.au/coag_meeting_outcomes/2009-04-30/docs/child_protection_framework.pdf, retrieved 28 May 2009.

Crisp, B., Anderson, M., Orme, J. and Green Lister, P. (2006) 'Assessment Frameworks: A Critical Reflection', *British Journal of Social Work,* 37, pp. 1059–1077.

Curtis, K., Roberta, H., Copperman, J., Downies, A. and Liabo, K. (2004) '"How Come I Don't Get Asked No Questions?" Researching "Hard to Reach" Children and Teenagers', *Child and Family Social Work,* 9, pp. 167–175.

Department for Children, Schools and Families (2000) Integrated Children's System Briefing Paper 1, London: DCSF.

Department for Children, Schools and Families (2006) *Care Matters,* Green Paper, London: The Stationary Office.

Department for Children, Schools and Families (2007) *Care Matters* White Paper, London: The Stationary Office.

Department for Children, Schools, and Families (2007) *Children Looked After in England Year Ending 31st March 2007,* available from http://www.education.gov.uk/rsgateway/DB/SFR/index.shtml.

Department for Children, Schools and Families (2008) *Care Matters: Time to Deliver for Children in Care,* London: The Stationary Office.

Department for Children, Schools, and Families (2008) *Multidimensional Treatment Foster Care in England (MTFCE) Annual Project Report,* London: HMSO.

Department for Children, Schools, and Families (2009) *Statistical First Release,* available from http://www.education.gov.uk/rsgateway/DB/SFR/index.shtml.

Department for Children, Schools and Families (2010a) *Follow-up to the Care Matters National Stocktake,* available from http://webarchive.nationalarchives.gov.uk/20100113205508/dcsf.gov.uk/everychildmatters/publications/documents/laefollowuptocaremattersnationalstocktake/.

Department for Children, Schools and Families (2010b) *Promoting the Educational Achievement of Looked-after Children: Statutory Guidance for Local Authorities,* London: DCSF.

Department of Community Services (DOC) (2007) *Outcomes for Children and Young People in Kinship Care,* Ashfield: Centre for Parenting and Research, available from http://www.community.nsw.gov.au/docswr/_assets/main/documents/researchnotes_kinshipcare.pdf, retrieved 9 July 2010.

Department for Education (DfE) (2010) *Munro Review of Child Protection: Terms of Reference*, London: DfE.

Department of Health (1996) *Focus on Teenagers: Research into Practice*, London: HMSO.

Department of Health (1999) *Me, Survive Out There?* London: HMSO.

Department of Health (2000) *Framework for the Assessment of Children in Need and Their Families*, Department of Health, Department for Education and Employment, Home Office. London available from http://www.dh.gov.uk/prod_consum_dh/groups/dh_digitalassets/@dh/@en/documents/digitalasset/dh_4014430.pdf, retrieved 6 January 2010.

Department of Health (2002) *Care Leaving Strategies: A Good Practice Guide*, London: Department of Health.

Desmeules, G. H. (2003) *Family Group Conferencing: A Decolonization Journey for Aboriginal Children and Families in Child Protection Services*, unpublished master's thesis, Royal Roads University, Victoria, British Columbia, Canada.

Dixon, J. (2007) 'Young People Leaving Residential Care: Experiences and Outcomes', in A. Kendrick (ed.), *Residential Child Care: Prospects and Challenges*, London: Jessica Kingsley Publishers.

Dixon, J. and Stein, M. (2002) *A Study of Throughcare and Aftercare Services in Scotland, Summary Report*, Edinburgh: Scottish Executive.

Doolan, M. (2009) 'Social Work and Youth Justice', in M. Connolly and L. Harms (eds), *Social Work: Contexts and Practice*, Melbourne: Oxford University Press, pp. 304–318, Ch. 22.

Doolan, M. and Nixon, P. (2003) 'The Importance of Kinship Care', *Social Work Now*, 25, pp. 12–20.

Doolan, M., Nixon, P. and Lawrence, P. (2004) *Growing Up in the Care of Relatives or Friends: Delivering Best Practice for Children in Family and Friends Care*, London: Family Rights Group.

Edelstein, S. B., Burge, D. and Waterman, J. (2001) 'Helping Foster Parents Cope with Separation, Loss, and Grief', *Child Welfare*, 80(1), pp. 5–25.

Edleson, J. L., Gassman-Pines, J. Y. and Hill, M. B. (2006) 'Defining Child Exposure to Domestic Violence as Neglect: Minnesota's Difficult Experience', *Social Work*, 51, pp. 167–174.

Edwards, M., Tinworth, K., Burford, G. and Pennell, J. (2007) *Family Team Meeting (FTM) Process, Outcome, and Impact Evaluation Phase II Report*, (March), Englewood, CO: American Humane Association.

Family Rights Group (2009) *Report Analysing the Results of a Freedom of Information Survey of Local Authorities' Family and Friends Care Policies*, London: Family Rights Group.

Fanslow, J. (2002) *Family Violence Intervention Guidelines*, Wellington: Ministry of Health.

Fantuzzo, J. and Lindquist, C. (1989) 'The Effect of Observing Conjugal Violence on Children: A Review and Analysis on Research Methodology', *Journal of Family Violence*, 4(1), pp. 77–94.

Farmer, E. (2009a) *Making Kinship Care Work, Adoption and Fostering*, 33(3), pp. 159–27.

Farmer, E. (2009b) 'Placement Stability in Kinship Care', *Vulnerable Children and Youth Studies*, 4(2), pp. 154–160.

Farmer, E., Moyers, S. and Lipscombe, J. (2004) *Fostering Adolescents*, London: Jessica Kingsley Publishers.

Farmer, E. and Moyers, S. (2005) *Children Placed with Family and Friends: Placement Patterns and Outcomes*, Report to the DfES: University of Bristol.

Farmer, E. and Moyers, S. (2008) *Kinship Care: Fostering Effective Family and Friends Placements*, London: Jessica Kingsley Publishers.

Farmer, E. and Owen, M. (1995) *Child Protection Practice: Private Risks and Public Remedies*, London: HMSO.

Farris-Manning, C. and Zandstra, M. (2003) *Children in Care in Canada: A Summary of Current Issues and Trends With Recommendations for Future Research*, Ottawa: Child Welfare League of Canada.

Ferguson, D. M., Boden, J. M. and Horwood, L. J. (2008) 'Exposure to Childhood Sexual and Physical Abuse and Adjustment in Early Adulthood', *Child Abuse and Neglect*, 32, pp. 607–619.

Ferguson, H. (2004) *Protecting Children in Time: Child Abuse, Child Protection and the Consequences of Modernity*, Basingstoke: Palgrave Macmillan.

Ferguson, H. (2005) 'Working with Violence, the Emotions and the Psycho-social Dynamics of Child Protection: Reflections on the Victoria Climbié Case', *Social Work Education*, 24(7), pp. 781–795.

Ferguson, H. (2010) 'Walks, Home Visits and Atmospheres: Risk and the Everyday Practices and Mobilities of Social Work and Child Protection', *Br J Soc Work*, 40(4), pp. 1100–1117.

Field, J. (2008) 'Rethinking Supervision and Shaping Future Practice', *Social Work Now*, 40, August, pp. 11–18, available from http://www.cyf.govt.nz/about-us/publications/social-work-now.html.

Finzi, F., Ram, A., Har-Even, D., Shnit, D. and Weizman, A. (2001) 'Attachment Styles and Aggression in Physically Abused and Neglected Children', [Electronic version] *Journal of Youth and Adolescence*, 30(6), pp. 769–786.

Fontes, L. A. (2005) *Child Abuse and Culture: Working with Diverse Families*, New York: Guilford Press.

Fox, A., Frasch, K. and Berrick, J. D. (2000) *Listening to Children in Foster Care: An Empirically Based Curriculum*, [Electronic version] Berkeley, CA: Child Welfare Research Centre.

France, A., Freiberg, K. and Homel, R. (2010) 'Beyond Risk Factors: Towards a Holistic Prevention Paradigm for Children and Young People', *British Journal of Social Work* (advance access), February 2010, pp. 1–19.

Friend, C., Shlonsky, A. and Lambert, L. (2008) 'From Evolving Discourses to New Practice Approaches in Domestic Violence and Child Protective Services', *Children and Youth Services Review*, 30, pp. 689–698.

Fulcher, L. (2001) 'Differential Assessment of Residential Group Care for Children and Young People', *British Journal of Social Work*, 31(3), pp. 417–435.

Furman, R. and Jackson, R. (2002) 'Wrap-around Services: An Analysis of Community-based Mental Health Services for Children', [Electronic version] *Journal of Child and Adolescent Psychiatric Nursing*, 15(3), pp. 124–131.

Gelles, R. (1982) 'Toward Better Research on Child Abuse and Neglect: A Response to Besharov', *Child Abuse and Neglect,* 6, pp. 495–496.

Geraghty, A., Laing, T. and Warren, J. (2002) 'Evaluating the Contribution of Residential Services', *Social Work Now,* 21, pp. 16–21.

Gibbs, J., Dwyer, J. and Vivekananda, K. (2009) *Leading Practice: A Resource Guide for Child Protection Frontline and Middle Managers,* available from: http://www.cyf.vic.gov.au/__data/assets/pdf_file/0008/414494/leading-practice-resource-guide.pdf.

Gilbert, N. (1997) *Combating Child Abuse: International Perspectives and Trends,* Oxford: Oxford University Press.

Gilligan, R. (2000a) 'Promoting Resilience in Children in Foster Care', in G. Kelly and R. Gilligan (eds), *Issues in Foster Care: Policy, Practice and Research,* London: Jessica Kingsley Publishers, pp. 107–126.

Gilligan, R. (2000b) 'The Developmental Implications for Children in Public Care: Irish and International Perspectives', *The Irish Journal of Psychology,* 21(3–4), pp. 138–153.

Golding, K. (2004) 'Providing Specialist Psychological Support to Foster Carers: A Consultation Model', *Child and Adolescent Mental Health,* 9(2), pp. 71–76.

Gray, M., Plath, D. and Webb, S. A. (2009) *Evidence-based Social Work: A Critical Stance,* London: Routledge.

Greig, A., Taylor, J. and MacKay, T. (2007) *Doing Research with Children,* 2nd ed, London: Sage.

Grevot, A. (2002) 'The Plight of Paternalism in French Child Welfare and Protective Policies and Practices', *Partnerships for Children and Families Project, June 2002,* available from http://www.wlu.ca/documents/7204/Grevot.pdf, retrieved 28 August 2004.

Groves, B. D. (1999) 'Mental Health Services for Children Who Witness Domestic Violence', *The Future of Children,* 9(3), pp. 122–132.

Grundy, E. and Henretta, J. C. (2006) 'Between Elderly Parents and Adult Children: A New Look at the Intergenerational Care Provided by the "Sandwich Generation"', *Aging and Society,* 26, pp. 707–722.

Gunderson, K., Cahn, K. and Wirth, J. (2003) 'The Washington State Long-term Outcome Study', *Protecting Children,* 18(1–2), pp. 42–47.

Halfon, N., Zepeda, A. and Inkelas, M. (2002) *Mental Health Services for Children in Foster Care, UCLA Centre for Healthier Children, Families and Communities,* 4, available from http://www.healthychild.ucla.edu/Publications/ChildrenFosterCare/Documents/Mental%20health%20brief%20final%20for%20distribution.pdf.

Hall, C., Parton, N., Peckover, S. and White, S. (2010) 'Child-Centric Information and Communication Technology (ICT) and the Fragmentation of Child Welfare Practice in England', *Journal of Social Policy,* published online by Cambridge University Press doi:10.1017/S0047279410000012.

Harding, L. (1999) 'Children's Rights', in O. Stevenson (ed.), *Child Welfare in the United Kingdom 1948–1998,* Oxford: Blackwell Science, pp. 62–76.

Harlow, E. (2003) 'New Managerialism, Social Services Departments and Social Work Practice Today', *Practice,* 15(2), pp. 29–44.

Hart, A and Lucklock, B. (2006) 'Core Principles and Therapeutic Objectives for Therapy with Adoptive and Permanent Foster Families', *Adoption and Fostering*, 3(2), pp. 29–42.

Hawkins, P. and Shohet, R. (1989) *Supervision in the Helping Professions*, Buckingham: Open University Press.

Healy, K. (2005) *Social Work Theories in Context: Creating Frameworks for Practice*, New York: Palgrave Macmillan.

Hek, R. (2007) 'Supporting Unaccompanied Young People in Foster Placements', in R. Kohli and F. Mitchell (eds), *Social Work with Unaccompanied Asylum Seeking Children: Practice and Policy Issues*, London: Palgrave.

Hek R., Aiers A., Morris, K. and Hughes, N. (2010) *Promoting Best Outcomes for Children and Providing Best Support for Carers: A Review of Selected Literature for Foster Care Associates*, Birmingham: FCA.

Herbert, M. and Wookey, J. (2007) 'The Child Wise Programme. A Course to Enhance the Self-confidence and Behaviour Management Skills of Foster Carers with Challenging Children', *Adoption and Fostering*, 31(4), pp. 27–37.

Herczog, M., van Pagee, R. and Pasztor, E. M. (2001) 'The Multinational Transfer of Competency-based Foster Parent Assessment, Selection, and Training: A Nine-Country Case Study', *Child Welfare*, 80(5), pp. 631–643.

Hetherington, R. (2002) 'Learning from Difference: Comparing Child Welfare Systems', *Partnerships for Children and Families Project, June 2002*, available from http://www.wlu.ca/documents/7203/Hetherington_Keynote_Address.pdf, retrieved 27 August 2004.

Higgins, D. J., Bromfield, L. M., Higgins, J. R. and Richardson, N. (2007) *Supporting Carers: Perspectives of Professionals from Aboriginal and Torres Strait Islander Organizations, Non-government Agencies and Government Departments*. Promising Practices in Out-of-Home Care for Aboriginal and Torres Strait Islander Carers and Young People: Strengths and Barriers, Paper 5. Australian Institute of Family Studies, Melbourne.

Higgins, M. and Swain, J. (2010) *Disability and Child Sexual Abuse: Lessons from Survivors' Narratives for Effective Protection, Prevention and Treatment*, London: Jessica Kingsley Publishers.

Hill, M., Stafford, A. and Lister, P. G. (2002) *International Perspectives on Child Protection*. Report on seminar held on 20 March 2002. Part of the Scottish Executive Child Protection Review: Protecting Children Today and Tomorrow. Centre for the Child and Society, University of Glasgow.

HM Government (2009) *The Protection of Children in England: Action Plan*, available from http://publications.dcsf.gov.uk/eOrderingDownload/DCSF-Laming.pdf, retrieved 15 January 2010.

Hogget, B. (1993) *Parents and Children: The Law of Parental Responsibility*, 4th ed, London: Sweet & Maxwell.

Holland, S. and O'Neill, S. (2006) '"We Had to Be There to Make Sure It Was What We Wanted": Enabling Children's Participation in Family Decision-making Through the Family Group Conference', *Childhood*, 13(1), pp. 91–111.

Holland, S. and Rivett, M. (2008) '"Everyone Started Shouting": Making Connections Between the Process of Family Group Conferences and Family Therapy Practice', *British Journal of Social Work*, 38, pp. 21–38.

Holland, S., Scourfield, J., O'Neill, S. and Pithouse, A. (2005) 'Democratising the Family and the State? The Case of Family Group Conferences in Child Welfare', *Journal of Social Policy,* 34(1), pp. 59–77.

Horwath, J. (2007) *Child Neglect: Identification and Assessment,* Basingstoke: Palgrave.

Horowitz, M. (2008) Family Conferencing as Core Child Protection Practice. Unpublished manuscript.

Howe, D. (2005) *Child Abuse and Neglect: Attachment, Development and Intervention,* Basingstoke: Palgrave.

Hughes, L. and Pengelly, P. (1997) *Staff Supervision in a Turbulent Environment – Managing Process and Task in Front-line Services,* London: Jessica Kingsley Publishers.

Hunt, J., Waterhouse, S. and Lutman, E. (2008) *Keeping Them in the Family: Children Placed in Kinship Care Through Care Proceedings,* London: BAAF.

Hunter, S. V. (2006) 'Understanding the Complexity of Child Sexual Abuse: A Review of the Literature with Implications for Family Counseling', *The Family Journal,* 14(4), pp. 349–358.

Huntsman, L. (2006) *Literature Review: Family Group Conferencing in a Child Welfare Context,* Ashfield: New South Wales Department of Community Services.

Hutchison, E. D. and Charlesworth, L. W. (2000) 'Securing the Welfare of Children: Policies Past, Present and Future', *Families in Society,* 81(6), pp. 576–585.

Ince, L. (1998) *Making it Alone: A Study of the Care Experiences of Young Black People,* London: BAAF.

Ironside, L. (2004) 'Living a Provisional Existence: Thinking About Foster Carers and the Emotional Containment of Children Placed in Their Care', *Adoption and Fostering,* 28(4), pp. 39–49.

Iwaniec, D. (1996) *The Emotionally Abused and Neglected Child: Identification, Assessment and Intervention,* Chichester: John Wiley & Sons.

Jackson, S. and Sachdev, D. (2001) *Better Education, Better Futures. Research, Practice and the Views of Young People in Public Care – Summary,* London: Barnardo's.

Jaffe, P., Wolfe, D., Wilson, S. and Zak, L. (1986) 'Similarities in Behavioral and Social Maladjustment Among Child Victims and Witnesses to Family Violence', *American Journal of Orthopsychiatry,* 56(1), pp. 142–146.

James, S. and Meezan, W. (2002) 'Refining the Evaluation of Treatment Foster Care', *Families in Society,* 83(3), pp. 233–244.

Jeffreys, H., Hirte, C., Rogers, N. and Wilson, R. (2006) *Parental Substance Misuse and Children's Entry into Alternative Care in South Australia, 2006.* Research Bulletin, Government of South Australia, Department for Families and Communities, available from: http://www.dfc.sa.gov.au/Pub/LinkClick.aspx?fileti cket=MKdXFK2RuXM%3D&tabid=811, retrieved 22 January 2010.

Johnson, B., Howard, S. and Dryden, J. (1997) 'Promoting Resilience in Children: Review of Literature and Research Plan', in N. J. Taylor and A. B. Smith (eds), *Enhancing Children's Potential: Minimising Risk and Maximising Resilience,*

Proceedings of the Children's Issues Centre, Second Child and Family Policy Conference, 2–4 July 1997, Dunedin.

Joseph Rowntree Foundation (2005) *The Experiences of Young Care Leavers from Different Ethnic Groups*, available from http://www.jrf.org.uk/publications/experiences-young-care-leavers-different-ethnic-groups.

Kadushin, A. (1992) *Supervision in Social Work*, 3rd ed, New York: University of Colombia Press.

Kapp, S. A. and Propp, J. (2002) 'Client Satisfaction Methods: Input from Parents with Children in Foster Care', *Child and Adolescent Social Work Journal*, 19(3), pp. 227–245.

Kendrick, A. (ed.) (2008) *Residential Child Care: Prospects and Challenges*, Research Highlights in Social Work Series, vol. 47, London: Jessica Kingsley Publishers.

Kiely, P. and Bussey, K. (2001) *Family Group Conferencing: A Longitudinal Evaluation*, Sydney: Macquarie University.

Knoke, D. (2009) *Strategies to Enhance Substance Abuse Treatment for Parents Involved with Child Welfare*. CECW Information Sheet #72E, available from: http://www.cecw-cepb.ca/sites/default/files/publications/en/SubAbuse72E.pdf, retrieved 22 January 2010.

Knutsson, K. E. (1999) *Children: Noble Causes or Worthy Citizens*, Aldershot: Arena.

Koch, M., Hilt, L., Jenkins, L. and Dunn, T. (2006) *Family Group Conferencing: 45 Children, A 12 Month Study*. Presentation at the World Forum: Future Directions in Child Welfare, Vancouver, British Columbia, Canada.

Kohli, R. (2007) *Social Work with Unaccompanied Asylum Seeking Children*, Basingstoke: Palgrave Macmillan.

Kost, K. A. (2001) 'The Function of Fathers: What Poor Men Say About Fatherhood,' *Families in Society: The Journal of Contemporary Human Services*, 82(2), pp. 499–508.

Kroll, B. (2007) 'A Family Affair? Kinship Care and Parental Substance Misuse: Some Dilemmas Explored', *Child and Family Social Work*, 12, pp. 84–93.

Laming, Lord (2003) *The Victoria Climbié Inquiry*. Report on an inquiry by Lord Laming, January 2003. Available from http://www.dh.gov.uk/prod_consum_dh/groups/dh_digitalassets/documents/digitalasset/dh_110711.pdf, retrieved 12 July 2010.

Laming, Lord (2009) *The Protection of Children in England: A Progress Report*, London: The Stationary Office.

Laws, S. and Kirby, P. (2007) *Under the Table or At the Table: Supporting Children and Families in Family Group Conferences – A Summary of the Daybreak Research*, Brighton and Hove Children and Young People's Trust.

Lawson, D. M. (2001) 'The Development of Abusive Personality: A Trauma Response', [Electronic version] *Journal of Counselling and Development*, 79(4), pp. 505–509.

Leve, L. D., Fisher, P. A. and Chamberlain, P. (2009) 'Multi-dimensional Treatment Foster Care as a Preventative Intervention to Promote Resiliency Among Youth in the Child Welfare System', *Journal of Personality*, 77(6), pp. 1869–1902.

Littlechild, B. (2000) 'Children's Rights to be Heard in Child Protection Processes: Law Policy and Practice in England and Wales', *Child Abuse Review*, 9(6), pp. 403–415.

Lohrbach, S. (2008) 'Group Supervision in Child Protection Practice', *Social Work Now*, 40, pp. 19–24, available online from http://www.cyf.govt.nz/about-us/publications/social-work-now.html.

Lohrbach, S. and Sawyer, R. (2004) 'Creating a Constructive Practice: Family and Professional Partnership in High-risk Child Protection Case Conferences', *Protecting Children*, 20(2–3), pp. 78–92.

Lonne, R., Parton, N., Thomson, J. and Harries, M. (2009) *Reforming Child Protection*, London: Routledge.

Luntz, B. K. and Widom, C. S. (1994) 'Antisocial Personality Disorder in Abused and Neglected Children Grown Up', *American Journal of Psychiatry*, 15(5), pp. 670–674.

MacDonald, G. and Turner, W. (2005) 'An Experiment in Helping Foster Carers Manage Challenging Behaviour', *British Journal of Social Work*, 35, pp. 1265–1282.

MacDonald, G. and Turner, W. (2009) *Treatment Foster Care for Improving Outcomes in Children and Young People (Review)*, The Cochrane Collaboration, London: Wiley.

Mackay, R. (2003) 'Family Resilience and Good Child Outcomes: An Overview of the Research Literature', [Electronic version] *Social Policy Journal of New Zealand*, 20, pp. 98–118.

Mackness, L. (2008) 'Improving Treatment Paradigms for Multi-abuse Domestic Violence Clients', *Te Awatea Review*, 6(2), pp. 4–6.

Mainey, A., Ellis, A. and Lewis, J. (2008) *Children's Views of Services: A Rapid Review*, London: NCB.

Malet, M. F., Mcsherry, D., Larkin, E., Kelly, G., Robinson, C. and Schubotz, D. (2010) 'Young Children Returning Home from Care: The Birth Parents' Perspective', *Child and Family Social Work*, 15, pp. 77–86. doi: 10.1111/j.1365–2206.2009.00645.

Maluccio, A. and Ainsworth, F. (2006) 'Family Foster Care: Development or Decline?' *Adoption and Fostering Journal*, 30(4), pp. 20–25.

Mannes, M. (2001) 'Reclaiming a Family-centred Services Reform Agenda', in E. Walton, P. Sandau-Beckler and M. Mannes (eds), *Balancing Family-centred Services and Child Well-being: Exploring Issues in Policy, Practice, Theory and Research*, New York: Columbia University Press, pp. 336–358.

Mansell, J. (2006) 'The Underlying Instability in Statutory Child Protection: Understanding the System Dynamics Driving Risk Assurance Levels', *Social Policy Journal of New Zealand*, 28, pp. 97–132.

Marie, D., Fergusson, D. and Boden, J. (2009) 'Ethnic Identity and Exposure to Maltreatment in Childhood: Evidence from a New Zealand Birth Cohort', *Social Policy Journal of New Zealand*, 36, August, pp. 154–171.

Marsh, P. and Crow, G. (1998) *Family Group Conferences in Child Welfare*, Oxford: Blackwell Science.

Martin, P. Y. and Jackson, S. (2002) 'Educational Success for Children in Public Care: Advice from a Group of High Achievers', *Child and Family Social Work*, 7, pp. 121–130.

Mayer, S. E. (2002) 'The Influence of Parental Income on Children's Outcomes', [Electronic version] Wellington: Ministry of Social Development.

McDonald, P. S., Burgess, C. and Smith, K. (2003) 'A Support Team for Foster Carers: The Views and Perceptions of Service Users', *British Journal of Social Work*, 33(6), pp. 825–832.

McFadden, E. J. (1998) 'Kinship Care in the United States', *Adoption and Fostering*, 22(3), pp. 7–15.

McIntosh, J. E. (2002) 'Thought in the Face of Violence: A Child's Need', [Electronic version] *Child Abuse and Neglect*, 26, pp. 229–241.

McKenzie, R. B. (2003) 'The Impact of Orphanages on the Alumni's Lives and Assessment of Their Childhoods', *Children and Youth Services Review*, 25(9), pp. 703–753.

McKeown, K. (2000) *Supporting Families: A Guide to What Works in Family Support Services for Vulnerable Families*, unpublished report, Dublin: Department of Health and Children.

McLeod, A. (2010) '"A Friend and an Equal": Do Young People in Care Seek the Impossible from their Social Workers?', *British Journal of Social Work*, 40, pp. 772–788, doi:10.1093/bjsw/bcn143.

Mech, E. V. (2001) 'Where Are We Going Tomorrow: Independent Living Research', in K. A. Nollan and A. C. Downs (eds), *Preparing Youth for Long-term Success: Proceedings from the Casey Family Program National Independent Living Forum*, Washington DC: CWLA, pp. 27–33.

Meltzer, H., Corbin, T., Gatward, R., Goodman, R. and Ford, T. (2003) *The Mental Health of Young People Looked After by Local Authorities in England: Summary Report*, London: HMSO.

Mennen, F. E. and O'Keefe, M. (2005) 'Informed Decisions in Child Welfare: The Use of Attachment Theory', *Child and Youth Services Review*, 27, pp. 577–593.

Merkel-Holguin, L., Nixon, P. and Burford, G. (2003) 'Learning With Families: A Synopsis of FGDM Research and Evaluation in Child Welfare', *Protecting Children*, 18(1–2), pp. 2 –11.

Ministry of Justice (2008) *Public Law Outline: Guide to Case Management in Public Law Proceedings*, available from http://www.justice.gov.uk/guidance/careproceedings.htm, retrieved February 2010.

Ministry of Youth Affairs, (2000) *Children in New Zealand: United Nations Convention on the Rights of the Child. Second Periodic Report of New Zealand*, Wellington: The Ministry.

Monds-Watson, A., Maanktelow, R. and McColgan, M. (2010) 'Social Work with Children When Parents Have Mental Health Difficulties: Acknowledging Vulnerability and Maintaining the "Rights of the Child"', *Child Care in Practice*, 16(1), pp. 35–55.

Morgan, R. (2005) *Being Fostered: A National Survey of the Views of Foster Children, Foster Carers and Birth Parents About Foster Care*, London: CSCI, www.rights4me.org.uk.

Morgan, R. (2006) *About Social Workers: A Children's Views Report*, London: CSCI, www.rights4me.org.uk.

Morris, K. (2007) *Camden FGC Service: An Evaluation of Service Use and Outcomes*, available from http://www.frg.org.uk/pdfs/Camden%20FGC%20Service.pdf, retrieved 28 February 2009.

Morris, K. (ed.) (2008) *Social Work and Multi Agency Working: Making a Difference*, Bristol: Policy Press.

Morris, K. and Burford, G. (2007) 'Working with Children's Existing Networks – Building Better Opportunities?' *Social Policy and Society*, 6(2), pp. 209–217.

Morris, K. and Burford, G. (2009) 'Family Decision Making: New Spaces for Participation and Resistance', in M. Barnes and D. Prior (eds), *Subversive Citizens: Power, Agency and Resistance in Public Policy*, Bristol: Policy Press.

Morris, K. and Featherstone, B. (2010) 'Investing in Children, Regulating Parents, Thinking Family: A Decade of Tensions and Contradictions', *Journal of Social Policy and Society*, 9, pp. 557–566.

Morrison, T. (1996) 'Partnership and Collaboration: Rhetoric and Reality', *Child Abuse and Neglect*, 20(2), pp. 27–140.

Morrison, T. (2001) *Staff Supervision in Social Care*, Brighton: Pavilion.

Morrow, V. (2004) '"We Are People Too": Children and Young People's Perspectives on Children's Rights and Decision-making in England', in M. Freeman (ed.), *Children's Rights*, Vol. II, Aldershot: Ashgate.

Moyers, S. (1995) 'Using Information Over Time', in H. Ward (ed.), *Looking After Children: Research into Practice*, London: HMSO, pp. 163–180.

Moyers, S., Farmer, E. and Lipscombe, J. (2006) 'Contact with Family Members and its Impact on Adolescents and Their Placements', *British Journal of Social Work*, 36, pp. 541–559.

Munford, R. and Sanders, J. (1999) *Supporting Families*, Palmerston North: Dunmore Press.

Munro, E. (2001) 'Empowering Looked-after Children', *Child and Family Social Work*, 6, pp. 129–137.

Munro, E. (2002) *Effective Child Protection*, London: Sage Publications.

Munro, E. (2007) 'Confidentiality in a Preventative Child Welfare System', *Ethics and Social Welfare*, 1(1), pp. 41–55.

Munro, E. (2008) 'Improving Reasoning in Supervision', *Social Work Now*, 40, August, pp. 3–10.

Munro, E. (2010) *The Munro Review of Child Protection. Part One: A Systems Analysis*, London: Department for Education.

Munro, E. (2011) *The Munro Review of Child Protection: Final Report. A Child-centred System*, London: Department for Education, available from www.education.gov.uk/publications/eOrderingDownload/Cm%208062.pdf.

Munro, E. and Parton, N. (2007) 'How Far is England in the Process of Introducing a Mandatory Reporting System?' *Child Abuse Review*, 16(1), pp. 5–16.

Nathanson, D. and Tzioumi, D. (2007) 'Health Needs of Australian Children Living in Out-of-home Care', *Journal of Paediatrics and Child Health*, 43, 10, pp. 695–699.

National Adoption Information Clearinghouse (NAIC) (2005) *The Long-Term Consequences of Child Abuse and Neglect*, available from http://www.childprotectionoffice.org/pdf/long_term_consequences.pdf, retrieved 8 July 2011.

National Children's Bureau (2010) *Healthy Care*, http://www.ncb.org.uk/healthycare/home.aspx?sve=783.

Neary, M. (2009) 'The Case for Care', *Public Policy Research*, 15(4), pp. 180–181.

Newall, P. (2005) 'The Human Rights Imperative for Ending All Corporal Punishment of Children', in S. N. Hart (ed.), with J. Durrant, P. Newell and F. C. Power, *Eliminating Corporal Punishment: The Way Forward to Constructive Child Discipline*, Paris: UNESCO.

Nixon, P., Burford, G. and Quinn, A. (with Edelbaum, J.) (2005) *A Survey of International Practices, Policy & Research on Family Group Conferencing and Related Practices*, Englewood, CO: American Humane Association.

O'Brien, V. (2000) 'Relative Care: A Different Type of Foster Care – Implications for Practice', in G. Kelly and R. Gilligan (eds), *Issues in Foster Care: Policy, Practice and Research*, London: Jessica Kingsley Publishers, pp. 193–213.

O'Sullivan, B., McKinney, A., and Gallagher, S. (2002) *Family Group Conference Pilot Project*, Belfast: North Western Health Board.

Odell, T. (2008) 'Promoting Foster Carer Strengths. Suggestions for Strengths Based Practice', *Adoption and Fostering*, 32(1), pp. 19–28.

Office for National Statistics (ONS). *Population: Adoptions*, available from http://www.statistics.gov.uk/cci/nugget.asp?id=592, retrieved 2 June 2010.

Office of the United Nations High Commissioner for Human Rights (OHCHR) (1989) *United Nations Convention on the Rights of the Child*, available from http://www2.ohchr.org/english/law/crc.htm.

Orme, J. G. and Buehler, C. (2001) 'Foster Family Characteristics and Behavioral and Emotional Problems of Foster Children: A Narrative Review', [Electronic version] *Family Relations*, 50(1), pp. 3–15.

Owusu-Bempah, K. (2010) *The Wellbeing of Children in Care: A New Approach for Improving Developmental Outcomes*, Abingdon: Routledge.

Park, J. M. and Ryan, J. P. (2009) 'Placement and Permanency Outcomes for Children in Out-of-home Care by Prior Inpatient Mental Health Treatment', 19(1), *Research on Social Work Practice*, January, pp. 42–51.

Parrott, L., Jacobs, G. and Roberts, D. (2008) *Stress and Resilience Factors in Parents with Mental Health Problems and Their Children*, Research Briefing 23, March 2008. Social Care Institute for Excellence.

Parton, N. (2006) *Safeguarding Childhood: Early Intervention and Surveillance in a Late Modern Society*, Basingstoke: Palgrave.

Pecora, P. J., Whittaker, J. K. and Maluccio, A. N. (1992) *The Child Welfare Challenge: Policy, Practice and Research*, New York: Aldine de Gruyter.

Pecora, P. J., Whittaker, J. K., Maluccio, A. N., and Barth, R. P. (2000) *The Child Welfare Challenge: Policy, Practice and Research*, New York: Aldine de Gruyter.

Pennell, J. and Anderson, G. (eds) (2005) *Widening the Circle: The Practice and Evaluation of Family Group Conferencing with Children, Youths, and their Families*, Washington DC: NASW Press.

Pennell, J. and Burford, G. (2000) 'Family Group Decision Making: Protecting Children and Women', *Child Welfare*, 79(2), pp. 131–158.

Perry, B. D. (1997) 'Incubated in Terror: Neurodevelopmental Factors in the "Cycle of Violence" Child Trauma Academy Version', in J. Osofsky (ed.), *Children, Youth and Violence: The Search for Solutions*, New York: Guildford Press.

Petrie, P., Boddy, J., Cameron, C., Simon, A. and Wigfall, V. (2006) *Working with Children in Residential Care: European Perspectives*, Buckingham: Open University Press.

Preston-Shoot, M., Roberts, G. and Vernon, S. (2001) 'Values in Social Work Law: Strained Relations or Sustaining Relationships?' *Journal of Social Welfare and Family Law*, 23(1), pp. 1–22.

Pryor, J. and Rodgers, B. (2001) *Children in Changing Families: Life After Parental Separation*, Oxford: Blackwell.

Quinton, D., Rushton, A., Dance, C. and Mayes, D. (1998) *Joining New Families: A Study of Adoption and Fostering in Middle Childhood*, Chichester: Wiley.

Rankin, D. and Mills, A. (2008) 'Establishing Health and Education Assessments for Children Entering Care', *Social Work Now*, 41, December, pp. 35–39.

Reid, W. and Epstein, L. (1974) *Task-centered Casework*, New York: Columbia University Press.

Rhodes, K. W., Orme, J. G., Cox, M. E. and Buehler, C. (2003) 'Foster Family Resources, Psychosocial Functioning, and Retention', [Electronic version] *Social Work Research*, 27(3), pp. 135–150.

Richardson, J. and Joughlin, C. (2002) *The Mental Health Needs of Looked After Children*, London: Gaskell.

Robinson, J. R. (2002) 'Attachment Problems and Disorders in Infants and Young Children: Identification, Assessment, and Intervention', *Infants and Young Children*, 14(4), pp. 6–18.

Rogers, J. [ed] (2003) 'New Directions in Child Welfare', in N. Trocmé, D. Knoke, and C. Roy (eds), *Community Collaboration and Differential Response: Canadian and International Research and Emerging Models of Practice*, Ottawa: Centre of Excellence for Child Welfare.

Rubin, D., Downes, K., O'Reilly, A., Mekonnen, R., Luan, X. and Localio, R. (2008) 'Impact of Kinship Care on Behavioral Well-being for Children in Out-of-home Care', *Archives of Pediatrics and Adolescent Medicine*, 162(6), pp. 550–556.

Ryburn, M. and Atherton, C. (1996) 'Family Group Conferences: Partnership in Practice', *Adoption and Fostering*, 20(1), pp. 16–23.

Salveron, M., Lewig, K. and Arney, F. (2010) 'Supporting Parents Whose Children Are In Out-of-home Care', in F. Arney and D. Scott (eds), *Working with Vulnerable Families: A Partnership Approach*, Melbourne: Cambridge University Press, pp. 227–245, Ch. 11.

Sandau-Beckler, P., Salcido, R., Beckler, M. J., Mannes, M. and Beck, M. (2002) 'Infusing Family-centred Values into Child Protection Practice', [Electronic version] *Children and Youth Services Review*, 24(9–10), pp. 719–741.

Sargent, K. and O'Brien, K. (2004) 'The Emotional and Behavioural Difficulties of Looked After Children. Foster Carers' Perspectives and an Indirect Model of Placement Support', *Adoption and Fostering*, 28(2), pp. 31–37.

Schofield, G. (2001) 'Resilience and Family Placement: A Lifespan Perspective', *Adoption and Fostering*, 25(3), pp. 6–19.

Schofield, G. (2002) 'The Significance of a Secure Base: A Psychosocial Model of Long-term Foster Care', [Electronic version] *Child and Family Social Work*, 7, pp. 259–272.

Schofield, G. (2003) *Part of the Family: Pathways Through Foster Care*, London: BAAF.

Schofield, G. and Beek, M. (2005) 'Risk and Resilience in Long Term Foster Care', *British Journal of Social Work*, 35, pp, 1283–1301.

Scott, D. (2006) *Sewing the Seeds of Innovation in Child Protection*, Paper presented at the Tenth Australasian Conference on Child Abuse and Neglect, Wellington, NZ. February 2006.

Scott, D. (2009) 'Early Intervention with Families of Vulnerable Children', in M. Connolly and L. Harms (eds), *Social Work: Contexts and Practice*, 2nd ed, Melbourne: Oxford University Press, pp. 262–274, Ch. 19.

Sellick, C. (2006) 'From Famine to Feast. A Review of the Foster Care Research Literature', *Children and Society*, 20, pp. 67–74.

Sellick, C. and Howell, D. (2004) 'A Description and Analysis of Multi-sectoral Fostering Practice in the United Kingdom', *British Journal of Social Work*, 34, pp. 481–499.

Sellick, C., Thoburn, J. and Philpot, T. (2004) *What Works in Adoption and Foster Care?* London: Barnardo's.

Selwyn, J. and Quinton, D. (2004) 'Stability, Permanence, Outcomes and Support. Foster Care and Adoption Compared', *Adoption and Fostering*, 28(4), pp. 6–15.

Selwyn, J., Saunders, H. and Farmer, E. (2008) 'The Views Of Children and Young People on Being Cared For by an Independent Foster Care Provider', *British Journal of Social Work*, advanced access online, pp. 1–20.

Sheehan, R. (2009) 'Social Work and the Law', in M. Connolly and L. Harms (eds), *Social Work: Contexts and Practice*, 2nd ed, Melbourne: Oxford University Press, pp. 334–344, Ch. 24.

Shlonsky, A., Friend, C. and Lambert, L. (2007) 'From Culture Clash to New Possibilities: A Harm Reduction Approach to Family Violence and Child Protection Services', *Brief Treatment and Crisis Intervention*, 7(4), pp. 345–363.

Shlonsky, A., Webster, D. and Needell, B. (2003) 'The Ties That Bind: A Cross-sectional Analysis of Siblings in Foster Care', *Journal of Social Service Research*, 29(3), pp. 27–52.

Shulman, L. (1993) *Interactional Supervision*, Washington DC: NASW Press.

Sieppert, J. and Unrau, Y. (2003) 'Revisiting the Calgary Project Evaluation: A Look at Children's Participation in Family Group Conferencing', *Protecting Children*, 18(1–2), pp. 113–118.

Sinclair, D., Wilson, K. and Gibbs, I. (2001) 'A Life More Ordinary: What Children Want from Foster Placements', *Adoption and Fostering*, 25(4), pp. 17–26.

Sinclair, I. (2005) *Fostering Now: Messages from Research*, London: Jessica Kingsley Publishers.

Sinclair, I. (2010a) *Stability and Well Being in the Care System*, NICE, http://www.nice.org.uk/guidance/index.jsp?action=download&o=47427.

Sinclair, I. (2010b) 'What Makes for Effective Foster Care: Some Issues', in E. Fernandez and R. Barth (eds), *How Does Foster Care Work? International Evidence on Outcomes*, London: Jessica Kingsley Publishers, pp. 189–203.

Sinclair, I., Gibbs, I. and Wilson, K. (2004) *Foster Carers: Why They Stay and Why They Leave*, London: Jessica Kingsley Publishers.

Slack, K. and Webber, M. (2007) 'Do We Care? Adult Mental Health Professionals' Attitudes Towards Supporting Service Users' Children', *Child and Family Social Work*, 2008, (13), pp. 72–79.

Smith, A. B. (1996) 'Opening Remarks' in N. J. Taylor and A. B. Smith (eds), *Enhancing Children's Potential: Minimising Risk and Maximising Resilience*, Proceedings of the Children's Issues Centre, Second Child and Family Policy Conference, 2–4 July 1997, Dunedin.

Smith, A. B. (1999) *Understanding Children's Development*, 4th ed, Wellington: Bridget Williams Books.

Smith, M. (2009) *Rethinking Residential Child Care: Positive Perspectives*, Bristol: Policy Press.

Social Policy Research Centre (2009) *A Framework of Practice for Implementing a Kinship Care Program*, Final Report for the Benevolent Society. University of New South Wales, July 2009. available from http://www.bensoc.org.au/uploads/documents/ImplementingAKinshipCareProgram.pdf, retrieved 8 July 2010.

Social Work Taskforce (2009) *Building a Safe, Confident Future: The Final Report of the Social Work Taskforce: November 2009*, available from: http://publications.dcsf.gov.uk/eOrderingDownload/01114–2009DOM-EN.pdf, retrieved 20 January 2010.

Spence, N. (2004) 'Kinship Care in Australia', *Child Abuse Review*, 13(4), pp. 263–276.

Spratt, T. (2001) 'The Influence of Child Protection Orientation on Child Welfare Practice', [Electronic version] *British Journal of Social Work*, 31, pp. 933–954.

Spratt, T. (2008) 'Possible Futures for Social Work with Children and Families in Australia, the United Kingdom and the United States', *Child Care in Practice*, 14(4), pp. 413–427.

Sprenkle, D. H., Blow, A. J. and Dickey, M. H. (1999) 'Common Factors and Other Non-technique Variables in Marriage and Family Therapy', in M. A. Hubble, B. L. Duncan and S. Miller (eds), *The Heart and Soul of Change: What Works in Therapy*, Washington: American Psychological Association.

Stanley, J. (2001) 'Child Abuse and the Internet', *National Child Protection Clearinghouse Issues Paper 15*, Melbourne: Australian Institute of Family Studies.

Staples, J. (2007) *Knowle West Family Group Conference Project: Evaluation Report*, Bristol: Barnardo's/Knowle West Neighbourhood Renewal.

State of Victoria (2001) *The Audit of Children and Young People in Home Based Care Services*, Service Development Unit, Child Protection and Juvenile Justice, Department of Human Services, available from http://www.cyf.vic.gov.au/__data/assets/pdf_file/0005/15692/home-based-care-audit.pdf, retrieved 25 June.

State of Victoria (2007) *Cumulative Harm: A Conceptual Overview*, Best interests series. Every Child Every Chance. Victorian Government Department of Human Services, Melbourne, Victoria.

Stein, M. (2002) 'Leaving Care', in D. McNeish, T. Newman, and H. Roberts (eds), *What Works for Children?* Open University Press: Milton Keynes, pp. 59–82.

Stein, M. (2004) *What Works for Young People Leaving Care?* Ilford: Barnardo's.

Stein, M. (2005) *Resilience and Young People Leaving Care*, York: Joseph Rowntree Foundation.

Street, E., Hill, J. and Welham, J. (2009) 'Delivering a Therapeutic Wraparound Service for Troubled Adolescents in Care', *Adoption and Fostering*, 33(2), pp. 26–33.

Sundell, K. (2003) *Family Group Conferences in Sweden – Continuing Social Services Programs for Children and Parents* [English Summary] from American Humane Association.

Sundell, K. and Vinnerljung, B. (2004) 'Outcomes of Family Group Conferencing in Sweden: A 3-year Follow-up', *Child Abuse and Neglect*, 28, pp. 267–287.

Swain, V. (2005) *Campaign Update*, Foster Care Issue 120, London: Fostering Network.

Takayama, J. L., Wolfe, E. and Coulter, K. P. (1998) 'Relationship Between the Reason for Placement and Medical Findings Among Children', *Pediatrics*, 101(2), pp. 201–207.

Taylor, C. and White, S. (2000) *Practising Reflexivity in Health and Welfare: Making Knowledge*, Buckingham: Open University Press.

Taylor, N. (2005) 'Physical Punishment of Children; International Legal Developments', *New Zealand Family Law Journal*, 5(1), pp. 14–22.

Terling-Watt, T. (2001) 'Permanency in Kinship Care: An Exploration of Disruption Rates and Factors Associated with Placement Disruption', *Children and Youth Services Review*, 23(2), pp. 111–126.

Thoburn, J. (1999) Trends in Foster Care and Adoption, in O. Stevenson (ed.), *Child Welfare in the United Kingdom 1948–1998*, Oxford: Blackwell Science, pp. 121–155.

Thoburn, J. (2007) *Globalisation and Child Welfare: Some Lessons from a Cross National Study of Children in Out of Home Care*, Norwich: UEA.

Thoburn, J., Chand, A. and Procter, J. (2004) *Child Welfare Services for Minority Ethnic Families: The Research Reviewed*, London: Jessica Kingsley Publishers.

Thomas, N. and O'Kane, C. (2000) 'Discovering What Children Think: Connections Between Practice and Research and Practice', *British Journal of Social Work*, 30, pp. 819–835.

Thorpe, D. and Bilson, A. (1998) 'From Protection to Concern: Child Protection Careers Without Apologies', *Children in Society*, 12(5), pp. 373–386.

Timms, J. and Thoburn, J. (2003) *Your Shout: A Survey of the Views of 706 Children and Young People in Public Care*, London: NSPCC.

Titcomb, A. and LeCroy, C. (2003) 'Evaluation of Arizona's Family Group Decision Making Program', *Protecting Children*, 18(1–2), pp. 58–64.

Tomison, A. M. (1995) *Spotlight on Child Neglect*, National Child Protection Clearinghouse Issues Paper 4, Melbourne: Australian Institute of Family Studies.

Tomison, A. M. (2002) *Preventing Child Abuse: Changes to Family Support in the 21st Century*, National Child Protection Clearinghouse, Issues Paper 17, Melbourne: Australian Institute of Family Studies.

Tomison, A. M. (2004) *Current Issues in Child Protection Policy and Practice: Informing the NT Department of Health and Community Services Child Protection Reviews*, National Child Protection Clearinghouse, Melbourne: Australian Institute of Family Studies.

Tremblay, R. E., Gervais, J. and Petitclerc, A. (2008) *Early Childhood Learning Prevents Youth Violence*, Montreal: Centre of Excellence for Early Childhood Development.

Trevithick, P. (2007) 'Revisiting the Knowledge Base of Social Work: A Framework for Practice', *British Journal of Social Work*, 38(6), pp. 1212–1237.

Triseliotis, J., Borland, M. and Hill, M. (2000) *Delivering Foster Care*, London: BAAF.

Trotter, C. (2004) *Helping Abused Children and Their Families*, Crows Nest: Allen and Unwin.

Turnell, A. and Edwards, S. (1999) *Signs of Safety: A Solution and Safety Oriented Approach to Child Protection Casework*, New York: W.W. Norton & Company.

UNICEF (2003) *A League Table of Child Maltreatment Deaths in Rich Countries*. UNICEF Innocenti report card, Issue No.5, September 2003.

United Nations (2006) *Conventions on the Rights of the Child (UNCROC)* available from http://www2.ohchr.org/english/law/crc.htm, retrieved 28 February 2009 .

US Department of Health & Human Services (2007) *Child Maltreatment 2007*. Washington DC: Administration for Children and Families, available from: http://www.acf.hhs.gov/programs/cb/pubs/cm07/index.htm, retrieved 23 January 2010.

Utting, D., Monteiro, H. and Ghate, D. (2007) *Interventions for Children at Risk of Developing Antisocial Personality Disorder: Report to the Department of Health and Prime Minister's Strategy Unit*, March 2007, Policy Research Bureau: London.

Victorian State Government (May 2008) *Every Child Every Chance. Best Interests Case Practice Model. Summary Guide*, available from http://www.cyf.vic.gov.au/__data/assets/pdf_file/0004/497965/best-interests-case-practice-summary-guide.pdf, retrieved 6 January 2010.

Walker, L. (2005) 'A Cohort Study of 'Ohana Conferencing in Child Abuse and Neglect Cases', *Protecting Children*, 19(4), pp. 36–46.

Walsh, F. (2008) 'Using Theory to Support a Family Resilience Framework in Practice', *Social Work Now*, 39, April, pp. 5–14.

Walton, E., McKenzie, M. and Connolly, M. (2005) 'Private Family Time: The Heart of Family Group Conferencing', *Protecting Children*, 19(4), pp. 17–24.

Ward, H. (2008) *Patterns of Instability in the Care System*, NICE, http://www.nice.org.uk/guidance/index.jsp?action=download&o=47426.

Ward, T. and Connolly, M. (2008) 'A Human Rights-based Practice Framework for Sexual Offenders', *Journal of Sexual Aggression*, 14(2), pp. 87–98.

Watkins, B. and Bentovim, A. (1992) 'The Sexual Abuse of Male Children and Adolescents: A Review of Current Research', *Journal of Child Psychology and Psychiatry*, 33(1), pp. 197–248.

Watson, S. (2005) 'Attachment Theory and Social Work', in M. Nash, R. Munford and K. O'Donoghue (eds), *Social Work Theories in Action*, London: Jessica Kingsley Publishers.

Watzlawick, P., Weakland, J. and Fisch, R. (1974) *Change: Principles of Problem Formation and Problem Resolution*, New York: Norton & Co.

Welbourne, P. (2002) 'Culture, Children's Rights and Child Protection', *Child Abuse Review*, 11(6), pp. 345–358.

Weld, N. and Greening, M. (2004) 'The Three Houses', *Social Work Now*, 29 (December) pp. 34–37.

Wheeler, C. E. and Johnson, S. (2003) 'Evaluating Family Group Decision Making: The Santa Clara Example', *Protecting Children*, 18(1–2), pp. 65–69.

Whelan, D. J. (2003) 'Using Attachment Theory When Placing Siblings in Foster Care', *Child and Adolescent Social Work Journal*, 20(1), pp. 21–36.

White, S., Pithouse, A. and Wastell, D. (2009) *Error, Blame and Responsibility in Child Welfare: Problematics of Governance in an Invisible Trade*, London: ESRC.

Whittaker, J. K. and Maluccio, A. N. (2002) 'Rethinking "Child Placement": A Reflective Essay', [Electronic version] *Social Services Review*, 76(1), pp. 108–134.

Wiggins, C., Fenichel, E. and Mann, T. (2007) *Literature Review: Developmental Problems of Maltreated Children and Early Intervention Options for Maltreated Children*, 23 April 2007. Office of the Assistant Secretary for Planning and Evaluation (ASPE) U.S. Department of Health and Human Services.

Williams, C. W. (2001) 'The Independent Living Program: Today's Challenge', in K. A. Nollan and A. C. Downs (eds), *Preparing Youth for Long-term Success: Proceedings from the Casey Family Program National Independent Living Forum*, Washington DC: CWLA, pp. 1–14.

Wilson, K., Petrie, S. and Sinclair, I. (2003) 'A Kind of Loving: A Model of Effective Foster Care', *British Journal of Social Work*, 33, pp. 991–1003.

Wilson, K., Sinclair, I., Taylor, C. and Pithouse, A. (2004) *Fostering Success: An Exploration of the Research Literature on Foster Care*, London: SCIE.

Winokur, M., Holtan, A., and Valentine, D. (2009) *Kinship Care for the Safety, Permanency, and Well-being of Children Removed from the Home for Maltreatment*, Fort Collins, CO: The Campbell Collaboration, Campbell Systematic Reviews 2009:1.

Wolin, S. J. and Wolin, S. (1993) *The Resilient Self*, New York: Villard Books.

Woodiwiss, J. (2009) *Contesting Stories of Childhood Sexual Abuse*, London: Palgrave Macmillan.

Worrall, J. (2001) 'Kinship Care of the Abused Child: The New Zealand Experience', *Child Welfare*, 80(5), pp. 497–511.

Worrall, J. (2009) *Grandparents and Whanau/Extended Families Raising Kin Children in Aotearoa/New Zealand: A View Over Time*, Grandparents Raising Grandchildren Trust New Zealand, available from http://www.raisinggrandchildren.org.nz/uploads/75791/files/GRGResearchReport_09.09.09.pdf, retrieved 9 July 2010.

Wulczyn, F., Kogan, J. and Harden, B. J. (2003) 'Placement Stability and Movement Trajectories', *Children and Youth Services Review*, 25(5–6), pp. 431–462.

Yegidis, B. and Weinbach, R. (2006) *Research Methods for Social Workers*, 5th ed, New York: Pearson.

Zetlin, A. G., Weinberg, L. A. and Kimm, C. (2005) 'Helping Social Workers Address the Educational Needs of Foster Children', *Child Abuse & Neglect*, 29(7), pp. 811–823.

Index